W9-BMN-415

PUT YOUR
BEST FOOT FORWARD

MEXICO
CANADA

PUT YOUR
BEST FOOT FORWARD

MEXICO
CANADA

*A Fearless
Guide to
Communication
and Behavior
NAFTA*

MARY
MURRAY
BOSROCK

IES
International Education Systems

Published by International Education Systems.

This publication is designed to provide accurate and authoritative information in regard to the subject matter covered. It is sold with the understanding that the publisher is not engaged in rendering legal, accounting or other professional services. If legal advice or other expert assistance is required, the services of a competent professional should be sought.

Information in this book does not necessarily reflect the official views of any government. References to organizations, publications and individuals are not endorsements. The author alone is responsible for errors of omission or commission in the contents of this book.

Library of Congress Publisher's Cataloging-in-Publication Data

Bosrock, Mary Murray.
      Put your best foot forward—Mexico/Canada: a fearless guide to international communication and behavior—NAFTA/ Mary Murray Bosrock.
      p. cm.— (Put your best foot forward; bk. 3)
      Includes index.
      Preassigned LCCN: 94-77283
      ISBN 0-9637530-5-3
      1. Mexico—Business etiquette. 2. Mexico — Intercultural communication. 3. Canada—Business etiquette. 4. Canada—Intercultural communication. Title. II. Series: Bosrock, Mary Murray. Put your best foot forward; bk. 3.

    E41.B67 1993   917.04'539
                                       QBI94-1422

Printed in the United States of America
10 9 8 7 6 5 4 3 2 1

In memory of my Father

who taught me through

his example that nothing

is impossible.

Look for other international education
products from IES,
including:

Put Your Best Foot Forward — Asia
Put Your Best Foot Forward — Europe
Put Your Best Foot Forward — Russia

Research and Production: Michael Trucano
Illustrations: Craig MacIntosh
Design: Brett Olson

TABLE OF CONTENTS

i.

ACKNOWLEDGMENTS

Thanks to the dozens of people—businesspeople,
diplomats, scholars and professionals—who have
drawn on their own experience and knowledge
to contribute ideas and observations to this
book, and especially to those who helped review
the manuscript. They include:

Brian Buckley, Consul General,
   Canadian Consulate General, Minneapolis
Paul Bennett, Consul, Canadian Consulate General,
   Minneapolis
Carrie Farrow
Hector Garcia, MEX-US Interinvest
Roy Garza, Executive Director,
   Spanish Speaking Affairs Council
Brent Hillier, CAE Vanguard
Diane Johnson, Spanish Speaking Affairs Council
Barb Mattson, International Trade Representative,
   Minnesota Trade Office
John G. Mott, Arthur Andersen
Bill Reid, President, CAE Vanguard
Mark Thompson, Arthur Andersen

*A special thank
you to John G.
Mott for explaining
NAFTA.*

And to all others who encouraged me in ways
large and small, my sincere thanks.

—*Mary Murray Bosrock*
St. Paul, Minnesota
Fall, 1994

ii.

INTRODUCTION

Before you read one word of this book, please understand that it reflects my experiences as an international businessperson.

All of us personalize our observations regardless of where we are in the world. A dozen people on a street corner in St. Paul, Minnesota will tell twelve different stories about the traffic accident they just witnessed. A dozen people in Toronto or Mexico City, Vancouver or Guadalajara will do the same.

This book is primarily based on my observations; I'm just "telling it as I see it." However, my knowledge of Mexico and Canada has been accumulated not only through personal observation and experience, but also through meetings with people— diplomats, doctors, lawyers, businesspeople, teachers and students—from all over North America.

THE WORLD ACCORDING TO ME

Thus, *Put Your Best Foot Forward—Mexico/Canada* is my attempt to convey not only what I have learned, but also what other people with a great deal of experience have passed on to me. *Put Your Best Foot Forward—Mexico/Canada* has some fundamental, country-by-country guidelines that will make your interactions with Mexicans and Canadians easier, more comfortable and more fun. They'll get you over some of the first cultural hurdles so you can establish productive business relationships—and eventually, I hope, friendships as well.

Can you survive without this knowledge? Of course you can. As a matter of fact, Mexicans and Canadians don't even expect you to have this knowledge. Can this information help you understand potential partners and customers in Mexico and Canada? Can it help you avoid misunderstandings? Can it help you communicate clearly and effectively what you really want to say? You bet it can!

If you are on your way to either Mexico or Canada for the first time, you are in for a real treat. If you travel often to either Mexico or Canada, you are very lucky. Regardless of how dynamic the business environment or spectacular the tourist attractions, it is always the people—tens and hundreds and thousands of unique individuals—who hold my interest and eventually win my heart.

FORMAT

Everyone who reads this book is busy. I've attempted to respect your time by organizing the book into easily accessible sections divided by country and behavior. The behaviors and attitudes discussed in Part I are the first, simplest and most basic rules for communicating with someone from another culture. In Part II, you'll find specific information on communication and behavior in Mexico and learn how Americans are viewed from the Mexican perspective. In Part III, you'll find the same type of information about Canada. The easy-to-read, quick-reference format of the individual chapters allows you to find the information you need in a matter of moments.

WHO SHOULD USE THIS BOOK?

Although it was designed primarily as a resource for businesspeople, *Put Your Best Foot Forward—Mexico/Canada* should be equally helpful for leisure travelers, students, teachers, people in the travel and hospitality industry, and hosts who regularly entertain Mexican or Canadian visitors.

Keep this book on your desk or tuck it in your suitcase. Before you meet or talk with someone from Mexico or Canada, you can quickly learn or review important information that will assist you in communicating effectively.

THE BOTTOM LINE

What you learn from this book will allow you to move beyond stereotypes and superficial concerns so you can get to the business at hand more quickly and easily. Learning and reviewing the information in *Put Your Best Foot Forward—Mexico/Canada* will lead to increased revenues and earnings for your company and will literally go to your bottom line.

iii.
WHAT IS NAFTA?

by JOHN G. MOTT

It is a peculiarity of modern life that many people living in large cities hardly know their next-door neighbors. Despite talk of a "global village," this kind of phenomenon can also be observed among nations. Citizens of the United States, in particular, tend to lack awareness of the languages, cultures and business procedures in countries just north and south of their borders.

It is not easy for most people to understand the nuances of other cultures.

Without a doubt, it is not easy for most people to understand the nuances of other cultures. As trade barriers erode, however, there is undeniable incentive to learn more. The North American Free Trade Agreement (NAFTA), which is being phased in gradually over 15 years, provides more than enough motivation for many business people. This agreement unites a trading bloc of 360 million customers.

> *Whether your interests are social, commercial or a mixture of the two, there are more than enough good reasons to develop your skills in transcending borders within North America.*

> *Canada and the United States do more trade than any other pair of countries in the world.*

Estimated annual expenditures in this continental trading partnership are $6.5 trillion—a figure that represents the largest, richest market in the world. So, whether your cross-cultural interests are social, commercial or a mixture of the two, there are more than enough good reasons to develop your skills in transcending the borders within North America.

North Americans are enjoying a new, promising era of freer trade, thanks in part to the passage of NAFTA. The seeds of this historic trade agreement were planted in the early 1980s, and trade among Mexico, the United States and Canada has been expanding steadily since then. The market-opening U.S.-Canada Free Trade Agreement helped pave the way. During the 1985 "Shamrock Summit," U.S. President Ronald Reagan and Canadian Prime Minister Brian Mulroney agreed to negotiate a free trade accord, and the agreement took effect four years later. Canada and the United States now do more trade—roughly $200 billion a year—than any other pair of countries in the world.

Forging an agreement with Mexico, however, proved to be a greater challenge. The barriers included major wage differences, a technology gap, extreme contrasts in basic infrastructure such as roads and telecommunications, and a highly protected Mexican economy. Mexico's culture also presented unique challenges, which this book addresses in an appealing and accessible format.

The prospect of being overwhelmed by the much larger U.S. economy was so daunting that it discouraged Mexico from negotiating a partnership for many years. As its oil revenues dropped, however, Mexico dramatically changed course in the mid-1980s, moving from a tightly controlled, closed economy to a more open one.

After several years of difficult negotiations, the United States, Mexico and Canada signed the NAFTA accord. By late 1993, the legislatures of the three countries approved the agreement. The trinational partnership officially began on January 1, 1994, and is now on course to eliminate most trade and investment barriers on the continent.

As of the year 2008, qualified goods and services should flow freely across North America. In the coming years, production and marketing of many goods will be a North American enterprise rather than a U.S., Canadian or Mexican endeavor.

NAFTA is on course to eliminate most trade barriers on the continent by 2008.

NAFTA is joining two highly successful economies with a developing economy. While Canadian and U.S. per capita income are not markedly different from each other, the U.S.

gross domestic product (GDP) is roughly $6 trillion—about 20 times the size of the Mexican economy, even though the U.S. population is only three times as large as Mexico's.

In Canada, the potential gains may seem small, partly because Canada has enjoyed most of the NAFTA-style trade benefits with the United States since 1989. While Canadian-Mexican trade has been modest, all three countries anticipate a hugely expanding, consumer-driven Mexican economy, one that is sure to stimulate demand for U.S. and Canadian goods and services. Mexico's increasing population, its growing middle class and large percentage of young consumers offer an enticing market.

Mexico offers an enticing market.

Mexico views NAFTA as a way to diminish its economic isolation and link up with its prosperous neighbors to the north. In trade blocs such as the European Union, wealthy countries have invested billions of dollars in poorer countries and have helped narrow the wage gap.

The benefits to the United States are many, with some of the advantages being immediate and others being phased in over several years. Roughly 50 percent of U.S. exports entering Mexico became duty-free on the first day that NAFTA took effect, and U.S. exports to

Mexico rose nearly 10 percent in the first three months of the agreement.

In the coming years, a wide range of U.S. agricultural products that were subject to Mexican tariffs and import-licensing requirements will benefit, as will high-tech products, pharmaceuticals, computer software and entertainment exports. Tariffs on remaining industrial and agricultural items will be diminished gradually. Moreover, U.S. banks, telecommunications, insurance, accounting and trucking firms will be able to participate fully in the Mexican services market while access to the Canadian services market improves even more.

NAFTA accelerates the recent trade initiatives that have opened Mexico to the point that it is now the fastest-growing major market for U.S. exporters. In the process, Mexico has surpassed Japan and is now the second largest market (after Canada) for manufactured U.S. exports. While NAFTA strengthens trade prospects in the United States and Canada, its effect on the Mexican economy is potentially enormous. Employment, wages and outside investment should grow dramatically, as should the Mexican GDP.

Canada and Mexico are the two largest markets for manufactured U.S. exports.

NAFTA rules, however, are complex, so it's essential to search for the best articles, books and experienced advisers to help you achieve your business goals. While the accord promises an era of free trade, the term "free" is a misnomer. Free suggests a lack of borders, duties or any other impediments. In reality, a preferential system of trade is unfolding.

Since each country has sensitive industries that are being protected, the phase-out of tariffs in certain industries will last well into the next decade. Furthermore, "rules of origin" define which goods are eligible for preferential treatment. Only those companies that invest in North American production—at the component and raw-material levels as well as in the production of finished goods—can reap the full benefits of NAFTA.

The impact of this trade agreement is reverberating throughout the Western Hemisphere and beyond. Latin American governments have begun introducing economic reforms, including the dismantling of trade barriers, in preparation for possible free trade with North America. Chile, for example, has formally asked the United States to begin negotiating a free trade agreement. Although still underdeveloped, Latin American markets, together with those of the Caribbean countries, represent approximately 450 million consumers.

The success of NAFTA is not going unnoticed across the Pacific Ocean. Citing overtures from nations such as Australia, New Zealand, Singapore and South Korea, Canada's trade minister has already asked that NAFTA be opened to other countries outside the Western Hemisphere.

Free trade is a global movement, and economic integration is widely perceived as the most efficient way to do business worldwide. In addition to NAFTA, trading blocs in various stages of development have emerged in Western Europe, Asia and South America. These agreements are binding nations together to spur economic growth, create jobs and improve living standards.

With business and cultural acumen, business people can take advantage of the expanding opportunities in Mexico, the United States and Canada. To succeed, one must begin by making a commitment to understanding the economies, industries, markets and cultures of these countries. The next steps are to create strategies, develop detailed plans, and implement those plans at the right time. Finally, one needs to perform follow-up reviews and monitor the new provisions of NAFTA as they are phased in.

In a global economy, those who lack the initiative or the skills to transcend borders are likely to be left behind. For those adventurous and informed enough to forge ahead, the forces

The success of NAFTA is not going unnoticed in other parts of the world.

In a global economy, those who lack the initiative or the skills to transcend borders are likely to be left behind.

of economic integration are creating great opportunities.

There are economic as well as personal rewards to be gained from engaging in international trade. *Put Your Best Foot Forward— Mexico/Canada* follows in the footsteps of its highly successful companions: *Put Your Best Foot Forward—Europe* and *Put Your Best Foot Forward—Asia.* These indispensable guidebooks help us take important steps toward developing a stronger appreciation of our international neighbors, their cultures and business traditions.

John G. Mott, based in New York City, serves as partner in charge of International Tax and Business Advisory Services—Americas for Arthur Andersen, one of the world's leading accounting and professional services firms.

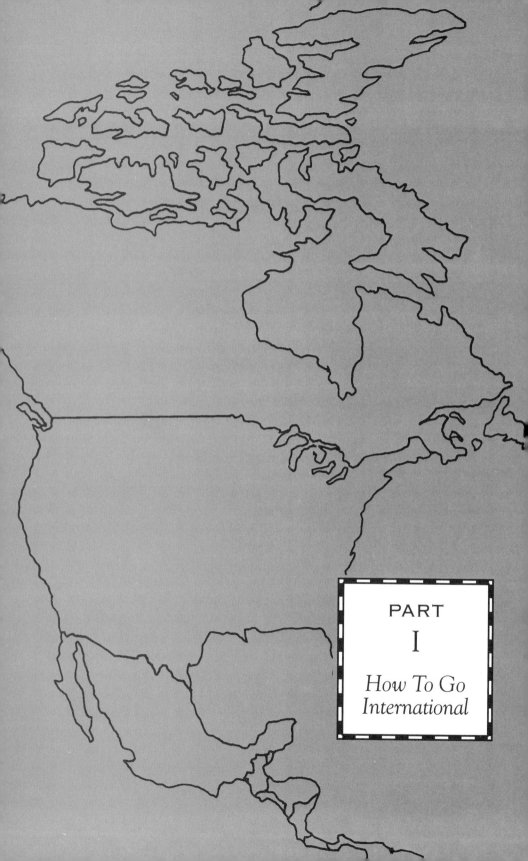

PART

I

*How To Go
International*

1.

THE UGLY AMERICAN

I have rarely met an "Ugly American"!

The term became widely known as the title of a 1963 movie starring Marlon Brando, based on a 1958 book by William Lederer and Eugene Burdick about an ignorant and incompetent U.S. ambassador to a fictional Southeast Asian country. It quickly became an epithet for rude, self-centered people who roam the world with utter disregard—even disdain—for other cultures.

Americans are uninformed— not ugly.

The Americans I know, work with and meet on my travels are quite the opposite. They want very much to understand and appreciate other customs and cultures. They're just uninformed—not ugly.

It isn't easy to understand other languages and cultures. We share this planet with nearly 6 billion people who speak 6,000 different languages. Obviously, most of us don't have the time or ability to learn dozens of languages or to become intimately familiar with scores of cultures. So how do we get started in this business of intercultural communication? By being flexible, open-minded, willing to learn and willing to make mistakes.

Trying to describe human behavior is tricky at best. No two people behave in exactly the same way; perhaps even more important, no two people interpret others' behavior in the same way.

Just about the time you're tempted to use stereotypes, you are reminded that each of the world's 6 billion people is unique. That's what makes going international so fun. Even though people look alike, speak the same language, eat similar food, practice the same religion and live in the same country, each and every person you meet will be different.

I have sat in homes, shops, offices and embassies with people of the same nationality and listened to them debate a particular custom or behavior. Women disagreed with men, older people disagreed with younger ones, and sometimes there was general disagreement. Only rarely did such a group reach consensus.

Consideration and respect are two of the qualities you most need to be a successful internationalist. It's so easy! You can't go wrong if you ask yourself, "Are my actions considerate and respectful of my foreign colleagues and their culture?"

Doing your homework before you visit a foreign country is essential. Once you're on the ground, there are some important ways to keep learning:

Observe what the local people are doing. This is one of the safest and easiest ways to establish appropriate behavior. Watch what others wear, how they greet each other, how they eat. Follow their example, and you'll usually be correct.

Listen actively and aggressively. Write down what you hear. When a person says his or her name, listen carefully and write down the phonetic pronunciation of the name. Listen for the title used. At social occasions, pay careful attention to what local people are saying to you and to each other. You'll learn a lot of things about their country and culture that will come in handy in future conversations, and you'll have many opportunities to ask informed questions.

Ask whenever communication or expected behavior is unclear. Ask your host or business associate, the concierge at the hotel, a clerk in a shop. Ask quietly and politely. You may feel

Observe the local people and ask informed questions.

a little foolish at first, but people will appreciate your interest.

We can learn a lot about appropriate behavior by observing, asking and listening. But especially in another culture, the ultimate learning technique is trial and error. We have to be willing to try new things, and we have to be willing to make our share of errors.

An ambassador I know says his wife always learns the language of a new country faster than he does. Why? Because she's not worried about making mistakes as she shops, tours, visits and dines. He, on the other hand—with an official position to uphold— never speaks the language unless he's certain that he'll be correct.

Sensitive imperfection can be endearing.

To try is to succeed.

There's a lesson in that story for all of us. We've got to be willing to take a chance—to make a mistake. It's important to understand that there are good mistakes and bad mistakes. Good mistakes are those that say clearly in any language, "I care, I'm trying, I'm sorry if I got it wrong." Sensitive imperfection can be endearing.

Try to speak a few words of someone's language, to taste the local food, to greet people properly, to learn others' behaviors and you will already have succeeded. To try is to show your vulnerability, your humanness. To try is to succeed.

Believe me, trying covers a multitude of errors! We all make mistakes when communicating in our own culture, so we certainly cannot expect to be perfect when communicating in a different culture. Remember, perfect is boring anyway! You never need to try for perfection— you just need to try.

You just need to try.

It's equally important to remember when interacting with people from other cultures that they too may be struggling to communicate with and understand us.

When we try, people understand that we're taking a risk, that we're making a special effort to reach out to them. They give us credit both for being willing to take the risk and for being willing to make the effort.

On such credit are new friendships—and new business relationships—built.

2.

VITAL STATISTICS

The most common negative comment made in other countries about Americans is that we're ethnocentric. Americans often appear to know nothing about anyone, anywhere else in the world, and, even worse, don't demonstrate much interest in learning.

In 1988, the Gallup organization conducted a survey for the National Geographic Society. The results were deeply disturbing: 14 percent of the Americans polled were not able to identify Canada on a world map, and 19 percent were unable to identify Mexico. From the results of their survey, Gallup projected that 24 million Americans were unable to identify Canada on a map of the world, and over 32 million Americans were unable to identify Mexico on a map of the world.

In the same survey, only 43 percent of Americans polled were able to state the

Faux pas

Not knowing basic facts about the country you're visiting isn't only ignorant—it's arrogant.

population of the United States as being between 150 and 300 million. When our North Americans neighbors were asked the same question about the population of the United States, a higher percentage of both Canadians and Mexicans answered correctly!

Going international requires having respect for the people you deal with—and respect means taking the time to develop at least a basic knowledge of your host country and the way your hosts live. Not knowing such basic facts when visiting a foreign country is not only ignorant—it's arrogant.

CHECK THE MAP, EH?

A Canadian diplomat recounts the story of a meeting with owners of small and medium-sized businesses at a trade show in Iowa. When asked if any of them were involved in foreign trade, only a few hands were raised. When asked if anyone did business in Canada, everyone's hand went up. "We don't consider our business with Canada to be foreign trade," explained one man.

3.

MEETING AND GREETING

The first impression is powerful! A good first impression creates the expectation of a positive relationship. A bad first impression, on the other hand, can be overcome only with a lot of work over a long period of time—and sometimes we don't get that chance.

Think about your own response to new people, especially in the work environment. Within a few minutes—maybe even seconds—most of us have developed a "gut feeling" about whether a new relationship will be positive or negative.

When you've traveled hundreds of miles to develop a new business relationship, you need to make the best possible impression in those critical first minutes. Your chances of creating a good first impression improve enormously if you've done your homework. Knowing what initial behaviors you're likely to encounter when meeting a person or group for the first time allows you to relax and project a positive image.

> *The first impression is powerful.*

Being prepared—and flexible—will allow you to react comfortably to the greeting offered. You'll also be well-served by restraint, common sense and good taste. The "Howdy, how y'all doin'?" greeting combined with a knuckle-breaking, arm-pumping handshake is not common outside of the United States and not likely to get a relationship off to a good start.

SOME GENERAL RULES FOR MEETING AND GREETING

- Always remove your gloves before shaking hands.

- Never shake hands with one hand in your pocket.

- Always use last names until invited to use first names.

4.
NAMES AND TITLES

For Americans who have been reared with a "Just call me Bill" attitude, the concern much of the world has about names and titles seems superficial.

Mexicans and Canadians know that the United States is a "first name" country. We shift from last names to first names almost on first meeting. We consider it warm, comfortable and friendly to do so, and think everyone else would like to do the same. But this is generally not the case in the rest of the world. Do not use first names until invited to do so by your host. Correct use of a person's name and title shows respect; incorrect use is an insult.

Do not use first names until invited to do so by your foreign counterpart.

Family history, rank and status are very important to Mexicans. Their names and titles are a source of pride, tradition and continuity.
Understanding and respecting this tradition is essential to making friends and doing business in Mexico.

Canadians are generally more reserved and formal than Americans, and are often put off by the "American rush" to use first names. Gauge your actions accordingly.

Just think of it as "The Comfort Zone." If your aim is to make your hosts comfortable—and amenable to doing business—respect their cultural comfort zone when it comes to using names and titles.

SOME GENERAL RULES ON USING NAMES AND TITLES

- Do your homework. Know the correct rules of name usage in each country.

- Do not use first names until invited to do so or until the other person repeatedly uses your first name.

- Ask each person by what name he or she prefers to be addressed. When in doubt, use a title. Err on the side of formality.

- Listen carefully to the pronunciation of the name when you're introduced to someone. Try to avoid having them repeat their names—but do so if it's absolutely necessary. It's better than getting it wrong.

- Ask for a business card so you can *see* the correct spelling and correct title. As soon as possible, jot down phonetic pronunciation of a name.

- Help your introducer or host with your name. Say your name slowly and pronounce it clearly.

Respect your foreign counterpart's cultural "Comfort Zone."

Rule of Thumb

Err on the side of formality.

5.
LANGUAGE AND
BODY LANGUAGE

The United States is one of the most
stubbornly unilingual of the major countries of
the world. Thankfully for most Americans,
English has evolved into the language of
international commerce. And because of our
shared historical and cultural developments,
the language barrier is seldom a hurdle when
doing business in Canada. Just because our
foreign colleagues can speak our language,
however, doesn't excuse us from not being able
to speak theirs, for to learn another's language
is one of the greatest of compliments. Nothing
bespeaks your interest more when in Mexico or
French-speaking Canada than taking the time
to learn their native tongues. Unfortunately,
most of us don't have either time or ability to
learn a new language at this stage in our lives.
If that's the case, at least take the time to learn
a few polite words and phrases in your
colleagues' native language. Your interest and
consideration will be rewarded.

*To learn another's
language is one of
the greatest of
compliments.*

Never mimic your colleagues' accents, pronunciations or manners of expression in English. If they're speaking in English as a courtesy to you, remember that they may be speaking in their second or third language. This may require a little extra listening effort on your part. If you get impatient, just think about how well you'd be expressing yourself in *their* native tongue! If there are ambiguities—linguistic or otherwise—ask politely for clarification. It's much better to ask a question than to court misunderstanding.

LONG LIVE THE POTATO

David, an American friend of mine, tells the story of one comic attempt to speak Spanish in Mexico:

A devout Catholic, David drove south from Minnesota to celebrate the papal visit to Mexico.

Overcome with emotion upon seeing His Holiness, David ran through the streets of Mexico City shouting "¡Viva la papa! ¡Viva la papa!"

David's newfound Mexican friend, while sharing in his excitement, thought it prudent to correct David's Spanish a little. "The Spanish word for 'pope' is el papa," the Mexican explained. "You're shouting, 'Long Live the Potato.'"

VIVA LA PAPA!

Language—what you say (and what you don't say!)—is just one form of communication. Researchers have determined that over 85 percent of interpersonal communication is nonverbal. Even if you are confident that you understand your foreign counterparts' words perfectly, if you misinterpret their body language (or allow them to misinterpret yours), you may not be communicating as well as you think.

So if an uncomfortable situation arises but you can't quite figure out what it is, it could be that, while your tongue is saying one thing, your body is communicating something else. Check the notes on body language in the Mexico and Canada chapters for guidelines specific to those countries.

BODY LANGUAGE

Misinterpreting body language can cause major misunderstandings.

Your tongue may say one thing while your body says another.

In his book Blunders in International Business, *David Ricks recounts some notable language blunders made by companies marketing their products in Quebec:*

One company advertised its lavement d'auto, *or "car enema," when what it really wanted to promote was its* lavage d'auto, *or "car wash." Another company identified its product as "used fresh milk," or* lait frais usage (*it wanted to claim "fresh milk used" or* lait frais employé). *A third company wanted to assert that its products were terrific, but instead said they were terrifying (*terrifantes). *Yet another company boasted its product was a "stumbling block to success" (it meant to say it was a "stepping stone to success").*

STUMBLING BLOCK TO SUCCESS

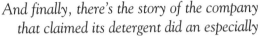

And finally, there's the story of the company that claimed its detergent did an especially good job on les parts de sale, *or the "dirty parts of the wash." Needless to say, the company was more than a little chagrined when it discovered that the phrase is French-Canadian slang for "private parts."*

The moral of the story: Faites vos devoirs! *(Do your homework!)*

USING AN INTERPRETER

Don't assume your communication problems are solved once you've hired an interpreter.

Don't assume your communication problems are solved once you've hired an interpreter (for the purposes of this book, we won't differentiate between translators and interpreters). In fact, they may just be starting. Some tips when using an interpreter:

• Make sure your interpreter speaks the appropriate language *as it is spoken where you're doing business*. Although they technically speak the same language, someone from Argentina or Spain may well not be familiar with many of the phrases and idioms used in Mexico City, for example.

- Discuss with your interpreter in advance the subject of the meetings and the main points you plan to make.

- Apologize to your colleagues for being unable to converse in their native tongue. Look at and address your remarks to your foreign counterparts, not the interpreter.

- Pause frequently to allow for interpretation— after every oral "paragraph" and, when the subject matter is especially important or complicated, after every sentence.

- Repeat your main points.

- Assume your counterparts can understand English, even if they are using an interpreter; never say anything you don't want others to hear.

- Follow up with a written summary of what was said and agreed upon.

Look at and address your comments to your foreign counterparts, not the interpreter.

Follow up with a written summary of what was said.

A large American car company learned the danger of translating without first getting sufficient local input. Introducing a new line of cars into the Mexican market, the American company was pleased to have decided on a name it considered both catchy and appropriate, the Caliente *("hot" in Spanish). Initial sales, however, inexplicably fell far below expectations. Inexplicable, that is, until company executives discovered that* caliente *is also Mexican street slang for a prostitute!*

TOO HOT TO HANDLE

6.
ON THE PHONE

The general attitude toward talking on the phone is different around the world. Many people from other countries simply can't understand how Americans are comfortable picking up the phone and immediately conducting important business with someone they have never met (and probably never will meet!). So be aware when calling internationally that, in many places, the phone is not used as extensively as in the United States.

The difficulties of communicating with someone from another culture are compounded greatly when trying to communicate over the phone. Not being able to see the person with whom you're talking makes non-verbal methods of communication impossible. The body language, gestures, pictures or written words that can help so much when interacting with someone from another culture aren't available to assist you. And if you don't speak the same language as the person you're calling, you might not be able to communicate *anything* effectively.

Always follow up an international phone call with a letter summarizing your conversation and what, if anything, was decided. Doing this can help you determine if a misunderstanding has occurred. This practice is especially important when speaking with someone for whom English isn't his or her native language (or when you're speaking a foreign language yourself).

Always remember that there is no substitute for talking face-to-face!

CALLING

Placing a call to another country can be an intimidating experience, especially when you don't speak the language of the place you are calling. Try to learn the words and phrases necessary to conduct a very basic conversation in the language of the place you are calling, or at the very least, be able to apologize for not speaking their language and ask if they can speak English (or connect you with someone who can).

In most countries, it is highly improper not to identify yourself first before asking to speak with a particular person. Whenever you are calling internationally, always remember to give the following information:

WHEN YOU'RE DOING BUSINESS IN CANADA OR MEXICO, ARTHUR ANDERSEN CAN HELP YOU TAKE GREAT STRIDES TOWARD SUCCESS.

Whether it's helping you solve the corporate complexities of doing business in Canada or Mexico, or helping your employees deal with everyday life in a foreign country, Arthur Andersen is ready.

We've been assisting companies establishing or expanding operations in Canada and Mexico for more than a generation. We can help you with a myriad of issues such as international tax planning, licensing, foreign tax credits, acquisitions and joint ventures, as well as human resources needs including developing and administering international compensation and benefits policies.

Our experienced professionals in a worldwide network of more than 300 offices in 71 countries share centralized training and a common methodology to assure you high standards and continuity of service across the region and throughout the world.

All of which will help you take giant steps toward reaching your goals.

John Mott, partner in charge
International Tax and Business Advisory Services
212-708-6012

Mac Gajek, partner in charge
International Executive Services
312-507-6810

ARTHUR ANDERSEN

ARTHUR ANDERSEN & CO, SC

When you take on the world, you're not alone.

You have the security of traveling with the American Express® Card, backed by all the services and people that come with it.

American Express® Travel Services Offices are your home away from home with over 1,700* travel locations in over 120 countries. There you can get a lost or stolen Card replaced usually by the end of the next business day with emergency Card replacement.

With the 24-hour Global Assist Hotline℠ you have a round-the-clock legal and medical referral service in the event of an emergency, when you travel 100 miles or more from home.

So use the American Express Card. You shouldn't have to take on the world by yourself.

Don't Leave Home Without It.®

- Greeting

- Where appropriate, apologize for not speaking the native language and ask if they speak English

- Your name (and title if appropriate)

- Your company

- Where you're calling from

- Who you would like to speak with

Example: Hello, my name is Carrie Farrow. I am the international marketing representative for IES and am calling from the United States. Could I please speak with...

ANSWERING

You should be aware that phones are answered in different ways around the world.

Don't be put off if someone answers the phone in a manner you consider impersonal or aggressive; that's probably just the way it's done in that particular part of the world. Some common ways of answering the phone may include giving all or part (or none) of the following information:

- Greeting
  Example: "Hello"

- Name
  Example: "Farrow"

- Company
  Example: "IES"

- Phone number
  Example: "227-2052"

7.

DINING AND
ENTERTAINMENT

Food is essential to the art of diplomacy. Your behavior at the table could make or lose foreign friends. When your hosts offer you a local delicacy or national specialty, they are offering you a sample of their culture as well as their friendship. They are giving you the best they have, and if you reject it, you are rejecting them, their culture and their friendship. This is not an auspicious way to begin a mutually beneficial relationship, so . . .

Eat what you're served—you may even like it! If you don't, eat a reasonable portion anyway. You'll survive, and eating what's in front of you just might seal the big deal.

Never joke, complain about or make a negative comment about the food you're served, and, if you are uneasy at the prospect of eating a certain dish, try not to let your discomfort show.

Food is essential to the art of diplomacy.

Rule of Thumb

Eat what you're served—you may even like it!

If you have a very weak stomach or really dislike a certain type of food, here are some tips to help you through dinner: Take a big gulp of the pink stuff (Pepto-Bismol) before you go. Don't chew particularly unpleasant food too much, just swallow fast—sometimes the consistency is worse than the taste. Eat slowly, and engage in conversation with your dinner partners—it will get your mind off the food and take up time until the next course is served. When offered seconds of something you don't like, say "Thank you, but let me be allowed to finish this portion first." If you're really afraid a particular dish might make you ill, decline politely; it is certainly preferable to gagging at the table.

TOASTING

Toasting can be an important part of dining with your foreign colleagues. Use toasts to establish closer, friendlier relationships. In Mexico or French-speaking Canada, make a toast in Spanish or French. Even if it isn't perfect, it will be enjoyed by your Mexican or French-Canadian colleagues. Keep your toasts short; an accompanying story (English is OK) is usually welcomed. Avoid telling jokes, which often do not cross cultural boundaries very well. Above all, enjoy toasting and being toasted.

Faux Pas

Avoid telling jokes.

Enjoy toasting and being toasted.

There is no place like home. Your city's best restaurants can't compare to an invitation to your home. Visitors always enjoy seeing how you live, how you decorate your home, what music and art you enjoy, and especially meeting your family. An invitation to your home is a special event not soon forgotten by your guests.

When entertaining foreign guests, always remember to check for dietary restrictions. Serve American-style food, but avoid huge, American-style portions of food. Resist the urge to feed tacos or enchiladas to your Mexican colleagues. Also, always ask your guests if there is a particular event or activity they would like to experience while in your city.

ENTERTAINING FOREIGN GUESTS

There is no place like home.

8.

TIPPING

Americans are among the most generous
people on earth. When Americans visit
another country and throw money at service
people, we're trying to be kind and
appreciative, not abrasive or arrogant. But we
often create the impression that we're
boorishly flaunting our wealth—or worse,
trying to take over the country!

Everyone has a sense of personal worth, and
that sense can be violated by a tip that's too
large or too small. The key is to know both
local customs and the value of what you're
giving. Not only do rules for tipping vary from
country to country, but inflation, fluctuating
currency exchange rates and rapidly changing
local attitudes all affect appropriate tipping.

In addition to the guidelines for tipping in
Mexico and Canada given in the respective
chapters, you are advised to ask a local
colleague or the concierge at your hotel for the

Rule of Thumb

*Know both local
customs and the
value of what
you're giving.*

current tipping practices—whom to tip, and how much. This simple step can save you considerable embarrassment—possibly in the presence of the local businesspeople you're trying to impress.

9.
DRESS

How you dress is a form of nonverbal communication. Dressing appropriately and attractively says to your hosts that you respect their culture and gives you the opportunity to make a positive first impression. How you dress is seen as an indicator of your personality and social status.

Good grooming is vital. Make sure your nails are clean and manicured and your shoes clean and polished. Never wear sloppy, dirty clothing. Shorts and jeans should be worn with caution. Always check to make sure they're appropriate. When in doubt, button up. Err on the side of being conservative. A dark suit and tie are always appropriate for a man, a nice dress or skirt and blouse for a woman.

Do not make the mistake of going native— or what you *think* is native. There is nothing that looks sillier or makes you more self-conscious than trying to look like a local and not succeeding.

Rule of Thumb

Err on the side of being conservative.

10.
GIFTS

Knowing when to give a gift and under what circumstances, what gift to give and to whom, and how to present a gift are vital parts of doing business abroad. Gift-giving customs vary depending on where you are, and observing the proper customs and etiquette is important. It would be a shame to end up insulting someone you're trying to impress.

In general, gifts should:

- Be of good quality and appropriate to the relationship and culture.

- Never be cheap or tacky, vulgar or insulting.

- Never be intimate or practical items.

- Be appropriately priced—neither demeaning nor extravagant.

- Be comparable in value to the gifts you receive.

Personalize a gift whenever possible. There is no nicer gift than one given because you took the time to listen and learn what someone enjoys—something that reflects his or her tastes, interests and personality.

GENERAL RULES FOR GIVING AND RECEIVING GIFTS

- When invited to someone's home for a meal, always bring a gift for the hostess. Small gifts to the host family's children are always appreciated.

- Always record the gift received on the back of the giver's business card, in your address book, or in a file.

- Write a thank-you note promptly.

- When you next see the giver, comment on the usefulness or your enjoyment of the gift you received. When appropriate, wear or display the gift given at your next meeting with the giver.

GENERAL RULES ABOUT BUSINESS GIFTS

- Do not initiate gift-giving if the recipient has nothing to give in return. If there are several people present, give everyone a gift, give a group gift, or wait until you are alone with the intended recipient to give your gift. Always save face for the giver and receiver.

- Tuck a wrapped gift into your briefcase. If you're then given an unexpected gift, you'll be able to reciprocate.

- Be aware that the U.S. government limits tax-deductibility to $25 on business-related gifts.

- Make sure that your gift is not interpreted as a bribe.

And remember: Always write down the gift you give so as not to give it to the same person a second time!

11.

THANK-YOU NOTES

Although the thank-you note was once a cornerstone of American civility, it's a custom that has fallen into widespread disuse in our society. It remains, however, a hallmark of culture and consideration, and is appreciated by any host or gift-giver. If he or she is a potential customer or business partner whose opinion of you is important, you'll find it's well worth a few minutes to write a thank-you note.

Always write a prompt thank-you note to anyone who is your host for dinner, who entertains you or who gives you a gift. Include a personal thought about the gift given or event attended.

Take your personal stationery with you when you travel, and try to write your thank-you notes before you leave your hosts' country. The correct name, address and spelling are more likely to be on hand immediately after an event—and can be checked, if necessary, before you leave the country. A thank-you note received soon after the gift is received or the event attended shows genuine appreciation.

> *It's well worth the few minutes to write a thank-you note.*

> *A prompt thank-you note shows genuine appreciation.*

12.
PUNCTUALITY
AND PACE

One of the greatest challenges you'll face in doing business internationally is understanding and accepting the local norms of punctuality and pace. It's important to understand that differences in such matters aren't necessarily good or bad—just different.

In a country like Canada, where punctuality is a habit, being late says to your hosts that you are:

- Lacking in respect for them.

- Sloppy or undisciplined in your personal habits.

- Potentially unreliable as a partner or supplier.

If you are an "Oh well, what's a few minutes late?" person, I strongly suggest that you become an on-time person when traveling abroad. Being "on time," however, means understanding and following local customs. What's late in Canada, for example, may well be early in Mexico. Don't get angry or upset if your Mexican colleagues are late for an appointment; they probably won't understand your anger, and will not feel guilty or apologize for being late.

Follow the guidelines in the Mexico and Canada chapters regarding specific attitudes toward punctuality in those countries. If uncertain, ask! Ask your host, a friend or the concierge at your hotel. It is always better to err on the side of punctuality.

Differences in pace are more difficult to understand and adjust to than differences in the sense of time. Pace deals with a sense of urgency (or lack of it), with making or postponing decisions, getting the job done, keeping promises and meeting deadlines. Differences in pace have their roots in deeply ingrained habits and attitudes—in culture itself. The local pace seems natural and right to the person performing the task. This is where knowledge and patience are vital to the success of your project—and your sanity.

13.
STRICTLY BUSINESS

In 1990, a major U.S. accounting firm surveyed CEOs of companies with $250 million or more in annual revenues. The companies agreed that the major hindrance to globalization is adapting to local cultures.

You have been asked by your company to go abroad. Someone thinks you have a skill worth exporting or an ability to sell your company in another land. You are entering the "international world," the world so many dream of and hope for but never get a chance to enter.

Are you lucky? You bet you are! Are you nervous? I hope so! Nervousness means you won't be arrogant—the worst potential downfall for the international business traveler. Arrogance means you're likely to say, "I am an American. I will do it my way. I'm paying the bill; let them adjust to me."

Nervousness means you might take the time and make the effort necessary to visit the library, read a few books on the countries you will visit, and, if necessary, learn a few basic phrases in their languages.

Cultural differences affect every facet of doing business. Recognize and respect these differences. To ignore these conventions is to risk offending your client and embarrassing yourself, your company and your country.

LA DIFFÉRENCE

When it first expanded into Quebec, a major American retailing chain learned the hard way to respect the province's cultural uniqueness. It launched a major marketing campaign using only English language materials. Québécois were put off by this aggressive anglophone invasion, the campaign flopped, and the American retailer had to move quickly to repair its reputation among French-Canadian consumers.

The chain paid the price for its cultural ignorance in other parts of Canada too: Company protocol required store employees to sing the Canadian national anthem every morning before work, give the company cheer and shout out the store number.
While Canadians are patriots, they are not flag-wavers, and the American retailer's dictated, American-style boosterism didn't sit well with them (in fact, most thought it all rather silly).

The moral of the story: It's bad business to allow the great similarities between the peoples of Canada and the United States blind you to the important cultural differences.

- Avoid a "U.S.-centric" mindset.

- Do not attempt to Americanize the workplace. Respect native customs and traditions. You will be far more successful if you adapt to the local culture. Respect the local work ethic.

- Show a sincere interest in people. Seek to build relationships.

- Localize your marketing effort. What sells in Manhattan doesn't necessarily sell in Monterrey and what sells in Monterrey doesn't necessarily sell in Montreal.

- An indigenous sales force is generally much more successful than a foreign one. Local people understand the market better and have better connections.

- Be flexible and willing to operate within the existing business and political structure.

- Be prepared for perception gaps. Ways of thinking and approaches to life and business may be different.

SOME GENERAL RULES

Rule of Thumb

Avoid a "U.S.-centric" mindset.

Localize your marketing effort.

Be prepared for perception gaps.

THE BUSINESS CARD

The business card is a very important communication tool and can be one of your most valuable resources when meeting people. The presentation of the card—and the receiving of your counterparts'—is one of your first opportunities to make a positive impression on the people you are meeting.

After shaking hands and introducing yourself (if you haven't done so already), look at the person and hand him or her your business card with your right hand. Be prepared to receive your counterpart's card. Always treat a business card with respect; don't shove it in your pocket or write on it in the giver's presence.

Always treat a business card with respect.

After your meeting, turn the card over and write on the back important information to remember about the person you met. You will be amazed when you write a thank-you note, speak on the phone, correspond or visit the person months later what this little card can help you recall. Your secretary will appreciate this information also.

A note of caution: Writing on a business card (especially during a meeting) may be offensive to some people. Do not write information on a business card until after the giver has departed. And never pass business cards out like you are dealing playing cards.

The "Hi, how are you? Let's sign the contract" approach rarely works outside the U.S. If you want the business, you'd better be prepared to take the time to personalize your relationships.

PERSONALIZING RELATIONSHIPS

- Phone, write, fax often; stay in touch. Make personal visits as often as possible—Americans have a reputation for disappearing.

Phone, write, fax often.

- Join appropriate associations in the local community. Contribute to local fund raising drives. Spend time on local issues.

- Make it clear you are in for the long haul. Take time to build confidence. Don't come on too fast or too strong. Adjust your pace, if necessary.

Adjust your pace, if necessary.

- Be yourself—be warm and friendly but initially more formal than you would be at home.

- Any knowledge you show about the local culture will be helpful to you in building closer and stronger business relationships.

SOCIALIZING

When establishing, renewing or continuing a business relationship in a foreign country, be prepared to socialize. This is no time for a "No, thank you." Remember that most people like to do business with people they know and trust. Time spent socializing will pay big dividends.

Be prepared to socialize.

When socializing:

- Respect local dining and drinking customs. Enjoy the local food—leave your diet at home. If drinks are being served, take one even if you only sip or pretend to drink it.

- Do not talk business at dinner unless your host initiates such conversation.

Be prepared for long evenings and late hours.

- Be prepared for long evenings and late hours. These may make or break a business deal.

14.
ESPECIALLY FOR WOMEN

As the new world order emerges, women worldwide are increasingly stepping forward to hold positions of power and prestige.

The prevailing attitudes toward working women are slightly different in each country. Prejudice exists in varying degrees all over the world. As a rule, however, following a few simple rules of behavior can make being a woman a decided advantage when doing business abroad.

Regardless of what the attitude toward women is in a given country, most foreign women are treated politely. Many of the resistant attitudes toward women are directed at local, not foreign women. As a woman working internationally, I have found being a woman an advantage. It is sometimes easier for a woman to get in the door to tell her story. Even in the countries where men prefer their spouses to be "seen and not heard," this attitude generally does not apply to foreign women. Also, many of the attitudes toward

Following a few simple rules of behavior can make being a woman a decided advantage when doing business abroad.

women are mainly reserved to perceived roles outside the workplace rather than in business.

GENERAL RULES FOR WOMEN

- Expect cultural misunderstandings over interaction between genders; try not to be judgmental. It may be new for some people to do business with women—be patient.

- Research local cultural habits toward women and, even if you think they are silly or antiquated, respect them.

- Establish your position and ability immediately. If possible, be introduced by a mutually respected person. Define your role clearly.

- Dress conservatively in a feminine style, but without flaunting your sexuality. Do nothing that can be misinterpreted as a sexual invitation or a come-on.

- Allow men to open doors, light cigarettes, etc. Try not to become embarrassed or angry if someone addresses you in a manner you consider too informal or kisses your hand. Roll with the punches.

- Aggressive "American-style" behavior is frowned upon in most countries. It is even more negative when exhibited by a woman. Never lose your cool.

15.

HEALTH AND SAFETY

When traveling abroad, it is imperative to check with a reliable, informed medical source to determine what precautions (if any) are needed for your trip.

If possible, visit a travel clinic—like those found at many university hospitals and major metropolitan medical centers. Many primary care physicians aren't familiar with current health problems in foreign countries.

If that's not feasible, call the Centers for Disease Control Fax Information Service at (404) 332-4565 and order the International Travel Directory, which will arrive on your fax machine within thirty minutes. Using the directory, you can order the documents appropriate to your trip. These documents will be delivered to you at no charge via your fax machine within an hour, and should give you and your doctor a good idea on how best to prepare for your trip.

Rule of Thumb

Check with an informed medical source to determine what precautions are needed for your trip.

Other good sources of information are the "Tips for Travelers" booklets published by the Department of State. Write to:

Superintendent of Documents
U.S. Government Printing Office
Washington, DC 20402

Specify the countries you're interested in. There is no charge.

And of course, the U.S. embassies and consulates in the countries you will be visiting will have up-to-date health information.

Check your medical insurance before you travel.

Check your medical insurance before you travel and make certain it covers emergency care in the places you'll be visiting. If it does not, take out a supplemental policy that does.

Pack a small first aid kit. Take your physician's phone number with you, as well as all prescription and non-prescription medication you may need. Keep the medication in its original, labeled containers to make customs processing easier.

SAFETY

Be sure to take all the safety precautions you would at home when traveling abroad. No matter how safe a city or a country is reported to be, there are potential dangers in any strange place.

Remember that the time to make important decisions is not after making a long journey on a crowded plane. Planning ahead and following these safety tips will substantially lessen the chances that your trip will take a turn for the worse:

- Arrange to have a local person meet you when you arrive, and when necessary escort you during your stay.

- Learn how to locate and use public telephones. Always keep the phone numbers and addresses of your company's local representative, your principal business contacts in the cities you are visiting and the nearest U.S. embassy or consulate.

- Learn the appropriate words and phrases in the local language so that you can communicate with non-English-speakers in an emergency.

- Never carry documents or packages that don't belong to you.

- Always carry your passport and other valuable items (airline tickets, important documents) on your person (not in a briefcase or purse) or put them in the safe of your hotel. Photocopy your passport and keep one copy in a place separate from your passport; bring along several extra passport photos. If your passport is lost or stolen, these materials will expedite the process of getting a new one.

Rule of Thumb

Be sure to take all the safety precautions you would at home when traveling abroad.

Learn how to locate and use public telephones.

- Conceal your valuables on your person, but do not wear a money belt or pouches outside your clothing or visibly hung around your neck—they could make you a target for theft.

- Do not set your bag down at your feet while checking schedules or using a phone.

HOTEL SAFETY

- Enter the hotel through the well-lit, main entrance. Take note of fire exits.

- Upon entering your room, check emergency phone numbers and test that the phone line to the front desk works.

- Secure your door whenever you are in your room by using all locking devices provided. Secure any sliding doors or windows and check locks on doors of any connecting rooms. Verify who is at your hotel door before opening the door.

Never leave cash or expensive jewelry lying around.

- Never leave cash or expensive jewelry lying around; put them in the hotel safe.

- Bring a little flashlight.

- Be especially careful in parking lots and ramps. Take advantage of an escort service if it's available.

16.
HOLIDAYS AND
FESTIVALS

Mexico and Canada (and many of the regions
within the two countries) have special holidays
and holy days on which businesses close. Also,
working hours may be different than those to
which you're accustomed. Check before you
schedule a business or pleasure trip to a
particular region. If you plan to drop in on
customers, meet with a colleague or shop in the
city, an unfamiliar holiday could ruin
your plans.

17.
THE TEN MOST COMMON
INTERNATIONAL GAFFES

Over the years I have assembled a list of mistakes Americans commonly make when going abroad. What's common practice in one area of the world may be absolutely taboo in another. Because of the great variety of customs, cultures and traditions, it's almost impossible to list specific acts that you should (or shouldn't) avoid.

With that in mind, here are ten types of gaffes commonly committed by Americans abroad:

1. ASSUMPTIONS

Making assumptions.

May include:

- *Assuming things are the same as at "home"*

- *Assuming you understand why things are different*

2. RELATIONSHIPS

Neglecting to develop relationships.

May include:

- *Trying to do business before developing a relationship*

- *Acting too informally*

- *Coming on too fast or too strong*

3. COMPARING

Comparing the place you're visiting to "back home."

May include:

- *Comparing customs*

- *Comparing the quality of goods or services*

- *Comparing business practices*

4. MONEY

Talking about money.

May include:

- *Talking about how cheap or expensive something is*

- *Talking about how much money someone makes*

5. BODY LANGUAGE
Misinterpreting body language.

May include:

- *Standing too close (or too far away)*

- *Smiling (or not smiling)*

- *Bowing (or not bowing)*

- *Making eye contact (or not making eye contact)*

- *Slouching*

6. FEET
Doing improper things with your feet.

May include:

- *Touching your feet or footwear*

- *Removing your shoes*

- *Showing the soles of your feet*

- *Moving an object or pointing with your feet*

7. HANDS

Doing improper things with your hands.

May include:

- *Touching someone*

- *Holding (or not holding) hands*

- *Shaking hands with a glove on or with your hand in your pocket*

- *Using the incorrect (usually the left) hand for a particular act*

- *Making an inappropriate gesture*

- *Touching an inappropriate area of your body*

- *Grooming (applying make-up, combing your hair, cutting your fingernails)*

8. DRESS

Wearing improper attire.

May include:

- *Dressing too informally*

- *Dressing immodestly*

- *Trying to "go native"*

9. NAMES

Using names incorrectly.

May include:

- *Using first names*

- *Neglecting to use a title (or using a lower title than appropriate)*

- *Mispronouncing a name*

- *Misspelling a name*

- *Calling someone by the wrong name*

10. EATING AND DRINKING

Neglecting to follow the appropriate dining customs and etiquette.

May include:

- *Exhibiting improper table manners*

- *Eating in public*

- *Showing displeasure with food or drink*

- *Declining an offer of food or drink*

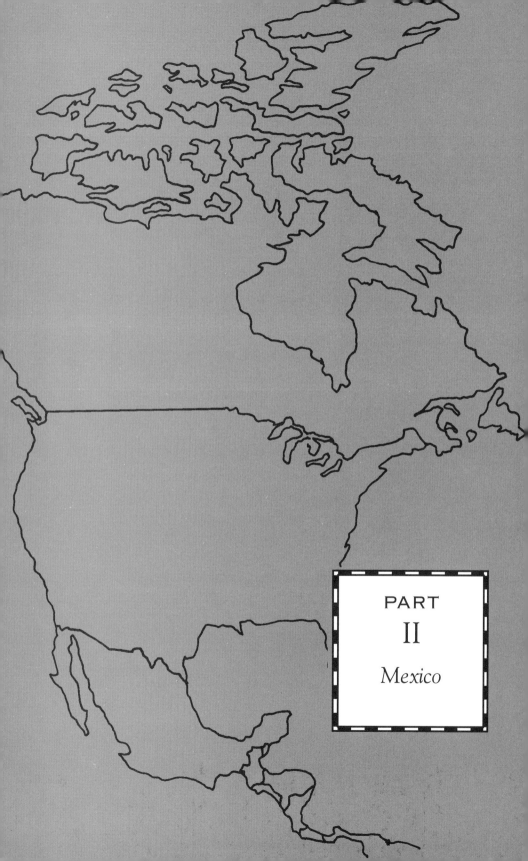

PART
II

Mexico

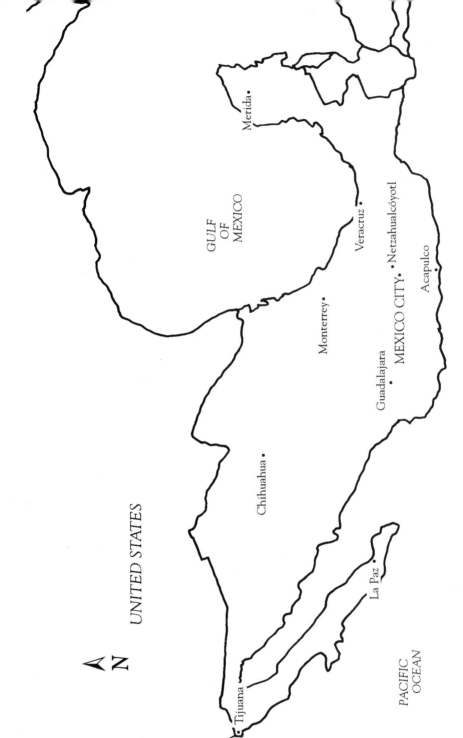

The boundaries and city locations of this map are not intended to be geographically accurate.

18.

LETTER FROM MEXICO

As I've collected material for this book, I've asked my Mexican friends how they view Americans and what points they'd like to make to Americans who visit Mexico. Here is a compilation of some of their more interesting and relevant comments:

Dear Friends from the United States:

You asked what we Mexicans think about you. Honestly, we like you and your country. We admire many things about you. You are open, friendly, optimistic, independent and filled with a "can-do" spirit like no other people in the world.

We admire the society and economy you have created. For many of us, *el Norte*, or "the North," represents opportunity and prosperity. You are world leaders in the aerospace, biomedical, pharmaceutical and telecommunications industries. Your physicians and medical facilities are among the best in the world. Your universities are excellent; many of our leaders have been educated in your institutions of higher learning.

As neighbors on the North American continent, our histories have been intertwined for hundreds of years. It is true that relations between our two great countries have had their ups and downs. "Poor Mexico," said Porfirio Díaz, a 19th century Mexican president, "so far from God, and so near the United States." But relations have been steadily improving. We are your third largest trading partner; you are our largest trading partner. Between six and seven million United States citizens visit Mexico every year. More than 400,000 U.S. citizens live in Mexico, and millions of people of Mexican heritage live in the United States. With the passage of NAFTA, our economies (and our fates) are bound to be linked ever closer.

Despite this, however, it often seems like we don't know each other very well.

We would like you to be our friends, but friendship must go both ways. If you wish to build a real relationship with us, you have to learn about what makes us who we are. You seem to respect the new and the young, while dismissing the old and traditional. We are very proud of our artistic and cultural heritage, a heritage that extends back

"Poor Mexico, so far from God, and so near the United States."

With the passage of NAFTA, our economies (and our fates) are bound to be linked ever closer.

thousands of years, and we ask that it
be respected.

When you come to our country, please don't
insist on trying to do things the "American
Way," assuming that what works in the
United States will work in Mexico. We may
not have as many ultramodern electronic
gadgets or fancy cars as you do, but that does
not give you license to tell us how things
should be done.

*Please don't insist
on trying to do
things the
"American Way."*

We are eager to embrace the new openness
across our borders that NAFTA has
introduced. However, we are likewise
vigilant to maintain the vibrancy and
uniqueness of our own culture. Through
American movies, TV, and music, we are
familiar with your culture. We are different.
Briefly stated, the land of *sol* is precisely that,
a land of the soul. The ferver of our faith
pulsates through every aspect of our life. This
fervor begins with our families, which is the
first concern of every Mexican, and extends
to relatives and firmly established friendships.

When we make plans we attach "God willing"
at the end because we know only too well
that fate lies not in our hands, but in His.
Come to Mother Mexico, enjoy our cuisine,
worship in our cathedrals, and rejoice at our
festivals and fiestas. And we'll tell you a
secret... the biggest key to revealing the

*We like to take the
time to get to know
the people with
whom we do
business.*

mystery of Mexico can be found under the cloak of Juan Diego... Roses, Roses, Roses and Our Lady of Guadalupe.

Sincerely,

Your Mexican Friends

19.
THE TEN
COMMANDMENTS OF DOING
BUSINESS IN MEXICO

1. Do your homework! A basic knowledge of Mexican culture and history will be richly rewarded.

2. Thoroughly research and know the background of the people or company with whom or which you intend to do business.

3. Develop and cultivate personal relationships before you sit down to do business. Business is usually done on the basis of relationships. Likability is the "magic wand." If people like you, they will forgive just about anything you do wrong.

4. Take your time and be patient. Plan to be in for the long haul. Relationships develop slowly.

5. Be flexible. Delays, canceled appointments and missed deadlines are par for the course.

6. Always be sincere. It shows. Sincerity is required to build trust. Trust is required to build a relationship.

7. Ask, look and listen! Mexicans are very proud of their culture and history and enjoy teaching others about their ways. A respectful interest will be appreciated.

8. Never act in a condescending or superior manner with your Mexican counterparts. There are few things that turn off Mexicans more than having American businesspeople enter their country, flaunt their wealth and act in a superior and patronizing manner.

9. Hire a reliable team of experts to take you into the Mexican market.

10. Assume the best about people and their actions. When a problem develops, assume miscommunication was the cause. Keep in mind that, if you are struggling to communicate with and understand Mexicans, they may be struggling to communicate with and understand you too.

20.

MEXICO
UNITED MEXICAN STATES

VITAL STATISTICS

POPULATION: 96 million (1994). Largest Spanish-speaking
                     country in the world. One-half of the population
                     is under 20 years old. Very high growth rate.
                     Largely (75 percent) urban.

CAPITAL: Mexico City, the largest urban conglomeration in
                     the world, with a population of around 20 million
                     (1994).

MAJOR CITIES: Guadalajara (3 million), Monterrey (2.3
                     million), Netzahualcótl (1.6 million).

LAND AREA: 756,006 sq. miles. One-fourth to one-fifth the
                     size of the United States, Mexico spans three
                     time zones. High central plateau. Mountains in
                     the west, south, and east.

GOVERNMENT: Federal democratic republic. Thirty-one states
                     and a federal district, Mexico City. The

president, who wields tremendous power, serves one six-year term and then must step down. Presidents usually pick their successor. Two-house Congress—a 64-member Senate and a 500-member Chamber of Deputies. Since 1930, Mexico has been ruled by the Institutional Revolutionary Party (PRI); in most cases the government and PRI are almost indistinguishable. In recent years, however, cracks have begun to appear in the PRI's dominance, and many now feel that Mexico is slowly (inexorably) on the way to becoming a multi-party democracy.

LIVING
STANDARD: GDP = US$3,872 per capita (1992). Second largest economy in Latin America.

NATURAL
RESOURCES: Petroleum, natural gas, iron ore, silver (world's leading producer), sulfur, lead, zinc.

AGRICULTURE: Corn, beef cattle, milk, wheat, coffee, beans, cotton, sugarcane, oilseed, cocoa.

INDUSTRY: Mining, motor vehicles, iron, steel, processed foods, tourism.

CLIMATE: The very dry areas of the northwest and north central desert regions have hot summers and mild winters. A moderate amount of rain falls on the northeast coast, where summer temperatures are warm and the winters are mild.

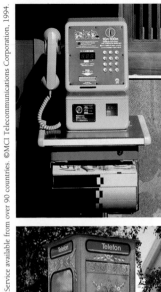

NOW YOU CAN TURN VIRTUALLY ANY PHONE IN THE WORLD INTO A WORLDPHONE.®

All you need to know is the WorldPhone* access number for the country you're in. Dial this access number, and you will get an operator who speaks English, and economical rates from overseas.

Call from country to country, or to the U.S., without intimidation or complications. No language barriers. No currency problems. No outrageous hotel surcharges.

For more information on WorldPhone, call 1-800-996-7535 in the U.S. or call the WorldPhone number from the country you're in.

WORLDPHONE
From MCI

Let It Take You Around The World.

Austria (CC)♦	022-903-012	**Italy** (CC)♦	172-1022	**Switzerland** (CC)♦	155-0222
Belgium (CC)♦	0800-10012	**Luxembourg**	0800-0112	**Turkey** (CC)♦	00-8001-1177
Canada (CC)	1-800-888-8000	**Mexico**▲	95-800-674-7000	**United Kingdom** (CC)	
Denmark (CC)♦	8001-0022	**Netherlands** (CC)♦	06-022-91-22	To call to the U.S.	
Finland (CC)♦	9800-102-80	**Netherlands Antilles** (CC)✛	001-800-	using BT†	0800-89-0222
France (CC)♦	19▼-00-19		950-1022	To call to the U.S.	
Germany (CC)	0130-0012	**Norway** (CC)♦	800-19912	using MERCURY†	0500-89-0222
(Limited availability in eastern Germany.)		**Portugal** (CC)	05-017-1234	To call anywhere other	
Greece (CC)♦	00-800-1211	**Russia** (CC)✛	8▼10-800-497-7222	than the U.S.†	0500-800-800
Ireland (CC)	1-800-55-1001	**Spain** (CC)	900-99-0014		

Use your MCI Card,® local telephone card or call collect...all at the same low rates. (CC) Country-to-country calling available. May not be available to/from all international locations. Certain restrictions apply. ♦ Public phones may require deposit of coin or phone card for dial tone. † International communications carrier. ✛ Limited availability. ▼ Wait for second dial tone. ▲ Available from LADATEL public phones only. All WorldPhone calls are subject to a $2.49 surcharge and per-minute rates.

Temperatures in dry central Mexico depend on the altitude; higher altitudes are generally mild, while the lower altitudes can be quite warm. Southern Mexico and the Yucatán are subtropical, with warm, wet weather year-round.

CURRENCY:

New peso. On January 1, 1993, the new peso was introduced at a rate of 1 new peso = 1,000 pesos. The old peso is gradually being phased out, but both currencies are still in circulation (they are pretty easy to tell apart). The dollar sign ($) is normally used to denote pesos; for documents traveling out of Mexico, however, Ps is normally used to avoid confusion. One peso is equal to 100 centavos. Bills come in denominations of 50, 100, 500, 1,000, 5,000 and 10,000 pesos, coins in 20 and 50 centavos and 5, 10, 20, 50 (two sizes, one for pay telephones) and 100 pesos.

THE PEOPLE

CORRECT NAME:　　　Mexicans.

ETHNIC MAKEUP:　　Largely Mestizos (a mixture of European—
predominantly Spanish—and Indian ancestry).
30 percent Indian, 9 percent European (largely
Spanish). "Indian" is more a cultural than a
racial designation. Mexicans identify themselves
as Mexicans first.

VALUE SYSTEM/
NATIONAL TRAITS:　　Mexicans place great value on personal relations
and relationships. One's private and family life is
most important. Schedules and deadlines are seen
as very general targets, and can be changed to
accommodate other, more important aspects in life.

---

*Mexicans place
great value on
personal relations
and relationships.*

Abstract things such as organizations, structured
plans and processes are not assigned as much
importance as human elements. Traits such as
directness and aggressiveness are not admired.
Ventures with high risk and high reward are not
as common as they are in the United States. The
Mexican concept of time is circular: One's
fortunes inevitably rise and fall through time, and
thus planning for tomorrow is not seen as important.

Mexico is a very class-conscious society, and
social stratifications are well-defined. Upper
class Mexicans will not dirty their hands with
tasks they find beneath them. Authoritarian
strains run through all aspects of society. Those

in positions of authority are not expected to make decisions by accepting input from colleagues, which is seen as a sign of weakness. To question an authority figure openly is viewed as questioning that person's character, and is not done.

In one sense, Mexicans are quite individualistic. They are very conscious of how they are perceived personally, and individuals take great pains to differentiate themselves from other Mexicans. This individualism, however, arises from a need to "fit in" and be respected by their particular group. The more positively a Mexican is perceived, the higher his or her standing in the eyes of his or her particular group or patron. It is from this respect from the group that Mexicans derive their sense of self-worth and power.

Mexican men are considered the most macho in Latin America.

Machismo plays a pervasive role in shaping Mexican culture. Macho attitudes are inculcated in Mexican males almost from birth, and Mexican society is male-dominated. Mexican men are considered the most macho in Latin America. Gender roles are strictly defined; women perform traditional roles.

In Mexico, the "truth" of a given statement must be understood in its particular context. For example, outsiders often misunderstand Mexican "promises." A promise may be made (1) as an expression of courtesy so as not to upset the party given a promise; (2) to save face for the person making the promise, who would not like to admit that the task is beyond his or her capabilities; and (3) because Mexicans feel the future is so difficult (or impossible) to predict, and thus whether or not the promise is actually carried out is in God's hands, and not the person's making the promise.

FAMILY:

The family is very important, and comes before all else. Mexican families, especially those outside the major urban areas, are generally quite large (often including extended families). The father is a strong authority figure, but the mother is in charge of the home. Due to the influence of the Roman Catholic Church, divorce is rare.

RELIGION:

Predominantly (90 percent) Roman Catholic (the state religion until 1911). Small number of Protestants, Jews, Native American religions. The Catholic Church is an important part of the culture and attitudes of all Mexicans. However, the church has little political influence.

EDUCATION:

Free schooling for first nine years. Children are required to go to school until they are fourteen. However, approximately 10 percent of Mexican children never begin school. Many members of the Mexican elite are educated at American and European universities. Mexicans receive an education firmly rooted in the classics; contemporary society is viewed in its historical context. 90 percent literacy rate.

SPORTS:

Soccer is the most popular sport. Baseball (especially popular in the north), bullfighting, basketball, tennis.

IMPORTANT DATES

900-1200   Toltecs rule area of modern Mexico.

1325   Legendary founding of the Aztec capital of Tenochtitlán.

1519   Spanish forces under Hernán Cortez defeat the Aztecs.

1521   Cortez establishes Mexico City on the site of Tenochtitlán.

1823   Mexican Republic declared.

1836   Texas becomes independent.

1845   The United States annexes Texas, sparking the Mexican-American War.

1848   The Treaty of Guadalupe ends the Mexican-American War, formally granting the areas of present-day California, Colorado, Nevada, Utah and Texas to the United States.

1857   New Mexican constitution adopted during presidency of Benito Juárez.

1864   Archduke Maximilian of Austria named emperor of Mexico after French invasion, rules for three years.

1876   Porfirio Diáz becomes president of Mexico, a position he holds with a few interruptions until 1911.

1910-20   Mexican Revolution.

1929	The National Revolutionary Party (PNR), the forerunner to the Institutional Revolutionary Party (PRI), formed and begins its one-party dominance of Mexican government.
1938	Mexican government nationalizes its oil industry.
1953	Mexican women granted right to vote in all elections.
1968	Summer Olympics held in Mexico City.
1982	Miguel de la Madrid Hurtado elected president of Mexico.
1988	Carlos Salinas de Gortari elected president of Mexico.
1994	The North American Free Trade Agreement goes into effect. Uprising in the southern state of Chiapas. PRI presidential candidate Luis Donaldo Colosio assassinated.
1994	PRI candidate Ernesto Zedillo Ponce de León elected president of Mexico.

- Shake hands or give a slight bow when introduced.

- Women often greet each other with a kiss on the cheek.

- Friends often greet each other with a hug.

- Bow when greeting a Mexican woman. Shake hands only if she extends her hand first.

- Common forms of address in Mexico are *Señor, Señora,* and *Señorita* (to be used for secretaries, females under eighteen, or when in doubt of marital status) followed by the family name. *Don* or *Doña* are terms of respect reserved for older Mexicans, and are followed by the first name.

- Status and rank are very important in Mexico. Address Mexicans with their titles and family name.

- Do not call Mexicans by their first name until invited to do so. First names are generally only used by good friends.

- Mexicans generally have two family names. The first is the father's family name; this is the official surname. The second is the mother's family name.

Rule of Thumb

Do not call Mexicans by their first name until invited to do so.

**Example: Juan Gutierrez Rodriquez.
Address as Señor Gutierrez.**

- Some Mexicans have hyphenated family names.

**Example: Jorge Campos-Garcia.
Address as Señor Campos-Garcia.**

- Mexican business titles don't correspond directly with American or Canadian business titles.

Mexican business title	American equivalent
director general	CEO
presidente	CEO
director	executive vice president
gerente	vice president, manager

- Address as *doctor/doctora* anyone who has a doctorate. An engineer is *ingeniero/a*, a professor *profesor/a*, a lawyer *licenciado/a*, a teacher *maestro/a*. *Licenciado* also designates someone with a university degree. *Maestro* is an especially prized title; many outside the teaching profession like to be addressed as *maestro*. Note that female titles normally end in *a*.

- Official language is Spanish. More than 100 Indian languages are spoken in Mexico; many Mexicans speak at least one Indian language in addition to Spanish.

- Any attempt to speak Spanish is appreciated by your Mexican counterparts, and is seen as a gesture of goodwill. But know your limitations—you could get yourself in hot water if you don't know what you're doing. It's best first to apologize for your deficiencies in the Spanish language before embarking on what may well be unintelligible to your Mexican colleagues.

Any attempt to speak Spanish will be appreciated by your Mexican counterparts.

¡NO COMPRENDO!

When you don't know the language, be prepared for some embarrassing situations—just ask Ronald Reagan! On a state visit to Mexico, the president gave a speech in English to a group of dignitaries in Mexico City. After he was finished, he sat down and listened to a speech in Spanish by a well-dressed Mexican man. This man's speech was regularly interrupted by applause—and a few times by laughter. President Reagan, not wanting to appear unfriendly, clapped and laughed along with the audience until politely informed that he was listening to a translation of his own speech!

- If you are familiar with Spanish, be aware that a certain word or phrase may have a different meaning in Mexico than it does in, say, Spain or Argentina. Also be aware that the Spanish spoken by Mexican-Americans often contains words and phrases not understood by those in Mexico. Beware of false cognates and words that have more than one meaning: Describing yourself as *embarazada*, for example, might mean you're a little red in the face, or it might mean you're pregnant!

- When speaking Spanish (or just trying to pronounce words in Spanish), never ever say "uh" or "um." These sounds do not exist in Spanish, and saying them makes your Spanish sound very American or Canadian (and not very pleasing to the ear of a native speaker). For example, *gracias* is pronounced "grah-see-ahs," NOT "grah-see-uhs." When in doubt, say "ah," never "uh." You'll be surprised at the difference this makes, and your Mexican counterparts will be pleased.

- In Spanish, letters in abbreviations are doubled to indicate plurals. Thus, *Estados Unidos* (United States) is abbreviated EE.UU.

- Differences in body language in the two countries often lead Mexicans to view Americans and Canadians as cold, and Americans and Canadians to see Mexicans as overly emotional.

- Mexicans generally stand close together when conversing. This takes some getting used to for many foreigners (you may want to practice). Don't show signs of discomfort, which would be seen as rude by your Mexican counterpart.

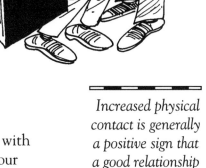

- Increased physical contact is generally a positive sign that a good relationship is developing. Mexicans often "hold" a gesture (a handshake, a squeeze of the arm, a hug) longer than Americans and Canadians do.

- "Thumbs up" means yes, good.

- Waving your hand from side to side with your index finger pointing up and your palm facing forward means "no."

- Mexicans usually beckon someone by pursing their lips and making a "psst" sound. Be aware that this common gesture is somewhat impolite.

Increased physical contact is generally a positive sign that a good relationship is developing.

- Always pass—never toss—an object. When paying for something, always place the money in the receiver's hand.

- Don't stand with your hands on your hips; this signifies anger. It is considered rude to stand around with your hands in your pockets.

- A very rude Mexican gesture is to make the "V for Victory" sign with your fingers, placing your nose in the wedge and covering your mouth with your palm.

- Most Mexicans are familiar with American gestures.

PHRASES

English	Spanish	Pronunciation
Good morning/day	*Buenos días*	BWAY-nohs DEE-ahs
Good afternoon	*Buenas tardes*	BWAY-nahs TAR-dace
Good evening/night	*Buenas noches*	BWAY-nahs NOH-chace
Hello	*Hola*	O-lah
Good-bye	*Adios*	ah-dee-OHS
Please	*Por favor*	por fah-VOR
Thank you	*Gracias*	GRAH-see-ahs
You're welcome	*De nada*	day NAH-dah
I'm sorry	*Lo siento*	loh see-ANE-to
Excuse me	*Perdóneme*	pair-DO-nay-may
Yes	*Sí*	see
No	*No*	noh
Pleased to meet you	*Encantado* (said by a man) *Encantada* (said by a woman)	ane-cahn-TAH-doh ane-cahn-TAH-dah
How are you?	*¿Cómo está usted?*	COH-moh ay-STAH oo-STED

MANNERS

Mexican cuisine is different from most of the "Mexican" food sold in the United States.

DINING:

- Mexicans may refer to the midday meal as either "lunch" or "dinner."

- Food (and lots of it) is a must for any social occasion. Alcohol may or may not be included at social occasions.

- Mexican cuisine is quite different from most of the "Mexican" food sold in the United States and Canada.

- Always keep both hands above the table.

- Don't leave the table immediately after you are finished eating.

- Don't eat while walking on the street.

DRINKING AND TOASTING:

- Drinking to excess is frowned upon in Mexico, especially when it's done by women. Hard, American-style drinking without food is normally reserved for the *cantinas*, from which women and children are usually barred. Social drinking by women is OK.

- Toasting is customarily done only by men in Mexico; foreign women normally shouldn't offer toasts.

Toasting is customarily only done by men in Mexico.

- Alcoholic beverages consumed in Mexico include beer, wine, brandy, mescal, pulque and the national drink, tequila.

- Tequila is distilled from one species of the spiny maguey plant (the *agave tequilana*, to be exact) which grows in abundance around the town of Tequila (which literally means "the rock that cuts"), located not far from Guadalajara. The infamous worm is added during bottling. Learn the proper five-step method for drinking tequila:

STEP ONE: Put your left hand in front of you like you're holding a can of beer.

STEP TWO: Carefully shake some salt onto the V-shaped area between your thumb and forefinger.

STEP THREE: Lick the salt.

STEP FOUR: Knock back a shot of tequila.

STEP FIVE: Bite into and suck on a wedge of lime.

After you've finished a bottle of tequila, Mexican drinking etiquette dictates that you swallow the worm at the bottom.

HOME:

- Mexicans are generous hosts. *Mi casa es su casa* ("my house is your house") is a national slogan.

- Never arrive early for a party.

- It's generally not a good idea for a foreigner to drop in at or stop by a Mexican home unannounced.

- On your first visit to a Mexican home, it is best to wear business attire unless specifically told otherwise.

- It is not necessary to eat every last bit of food on your plate.

- While a *gracias* when leaving and a short telephone call later expressing your thanks are normally sufficient, a short thank-you note is always appreciated.

TIPPING:

- Tipping is very common in Mexico.

- Restaurant: a 15 percent service charge is generally included in the bill.

- Waiters: 10-15 percent (even if a service charge is included).

- Haircutters: 10 percent.

- Porter: About half an American dollar a bag in pesos.

- Taxis: Half an American dollar or peso equivalent.

- Chambermaids: One American dollar a day or peso equivalent.

- Ushers/gas station attendants/bathroom attendant: Half an American dollar or peso equivalent.

American dollars are appreciated.

- American dollars are very appreciated.

- Men should always wear a shirt and tie, except at casual affairs.

DRESS

- Generally speaking, Mexican professionals dress better and with more style than their American and Canadian (Quebec excluded) counterparts.

- Always consider the climate when picking out your wardrobe (the high altitudes of Mexico City can make for some very chilly mornings, for example).

Rule of Thumb

Always consider the climate when selecting your wardrobe.

BUSINESS:
- Men: Conservative business suit.

- Women: Conservative business outfit. Make-up should always be worn.

- Recommended colors are navy and dark gray.

RESTAURANT:
- Men: Business suit.

- Women: Business outfit or nice evening wear.

CASUAL:
- Men: Shirt and pants.

- Women: Skirt and blouse.

- Shorts are only to be worn at a resort. Jeans are not normally considered appropriate casual wear.

HOLY PLACES:
- Always dress modestly and conservatively when visiting a religious site.

- Do not wear: Shorts, tank-tops, short skirts, etc.

Always dress modestly when visiting a religious site.

WRAPPING:

- Gift-wrapping in Mexico is similar to that in the United States and Canada.

HOSTESS:

- Flowers should always be given when visiting a Mexican home. It's OK to have them sent beforehand, or to bring them with you. If you have them sent, make sure that they arrive before you do!

- Give: White flowers, which are thought to be uplifting.

- Don't give: Red flowers, which Mexican superstition hold to be an agent for casting evil spells; yellow flowers, which are associated with death; marigolds, which are used to decorate grave sites.

BUSINESS:

- While gift-giving is not always a necessity when doing business in Mexico, gifts are recommended (and very appreciated!).

- Suggested initial gifts: Non-personal items with your corporate logo.

- Suggested gifts for subsequent meetings: items dealing with art and culture (art,

GIFTS

Flowers should be given when visiting a Mexican home.

books, music), upscale cigarette lighters, expensive pen sets, scotch, French wine, silk ties, imported chocolates.

DON'T GIVE:

- Knives and letter openers (which symbolize the severing of friendship), literature or artwork from Spain (they're Mexicans, not Spaniards!), handkerchiefs (associated with grief).

HELPFUL HINTS

DO:

- Be careful when using the words "America" or "American" (see below for more details).

AMERICA

Citizens of the United States should be aware of the significance of the words "America" and "Americans" to many in Mexico. The word "America," of course, comes from Amerigo Vespucci, the intrepid Italian explorer of the Western hemisphere, and all inhabitants of North, Central and South America are technically "Americans." Some Mexicans may take offense at citizens of the United States who refer to themselves as "Americans" and their country as "America," feeling that these terms apply just as accurately south of the Rio Grande (which, of course, they do). Although also technically inappropriate, "North American" is often seen as less offensive (even though Mexico, of course, is also part of North America).

That said, Mexicans themselves refer to citizens of the United States as americanos *or* norteamericanos. *Although a specific word does exist in Mexican Spanish to label someone from the United States very accurately—*estaunidense *("United States citizen")—it is more commonly used when writing, not when speaking.*

Those who identify themselves as "Americans" should be aware of the word's significance to Mexicans and be prepared to use such phrases as "an American (or North American) from the United States."

- Show a knowledge and appreciation of Mexican culture, which will win you friends.

- Be aware that Mexicans are very proud of their independence, and have a very strong sense of national identity and pride. Be conscious of resentment toward American imperialism and the North American sense of superiority.

- Try to speak at least a little Spanish!

- Always show great respect and deference to the elderly.

- Note differences in class and status in Mexico, for such differences are important. Comparatively speaking, Mexican actions and attitudes are often determined by the

Show a knowledge and appreciation of Mexican culture.

Try to speak at least a little Spanish!

differences between people (age, socio-economic status, gender, etc.), whereas Americans and Canadians do their best to pretend such divisions don't exist.

- Be aware that dates are abbreviated in Mexico with the day first, followed by the month and the year.

  Example: May 6, 1992 is written 6/5/92 or 6/V/92.

- Know that Mexico uses the metric system.

- The international dialing code for Mexico is 52. The area code for Mexico City is 5, Monterrey 83 and Guadalajara 36. To speak with an English-speaking international operator when in Mexico, dial 09. To call the United States directly from Mexico, dial 95.

DO NOT:

- Do not show any sense of condescension toward Mexico or Mexicans. Do not compare Mexico with the United States.

- Do not bring up such topics as illegal immigration into the United States from Mexico, the United States' annexation of the southwest, etc.

- Do not neglect the little things. Little things count! Not saying good-bye, for

Faux pas

Do not neglect the little things.

example, may well offend and adversely affect your relationship to a much greater extent than it would in the United States.

- Mexicans take great pride in their Indian heritage and indigenous cultures. Never say anything negative about Indians or their cultures.

- Punctuality is expected of foreign businesspeople. Your Mexican counterpart may be late or keep you waiting. Thirty minutes past the scheduled meeting time is considered punctual by Mexicans. Accept this—don't get angry. Remain flexible, for appointments are often delayed or canceled (and sometimes forgotten!).

- The traffic in Mexico City is truly horrendous, so prepare for unexpected delays.

- Never show up on time for a social engagement—you will be the only one who does, and will most likely be waiting for a very long time (possibly hours). It is best to ask guidance about when to actually arrive.

- Sometimes times are stated *a la americana, a la gringa,* or *la hora americana,* which means that an exact, American- or Canadian-type punctuality is expected, or *a la mexicana* or *la hora mexicana,* which implies a much more relaxed attitude toward time.

PUNCTUALITY

Punctuality is expected of foreign business people.

Never show up on time for a social engagement.

STRICTLY
BUSINESS

BUSINESS CARDS:

- Business cards are commonly exchanged in Mexico after initial introductions. There is no particular protocol for this procedure.

- Business cards should be printed in English on one side, Spanish on the other. Your college degree(s) should follow your name.

LANGUAGE:

Spanish is the language of business. English is widely understood by businesspeople.

- Spanish is the language of business. You should conduct business in Spanish whenever possible. You may need to hire an interpreter (preferably a native speaker who understands the language as it is spoken in Mexico). Ask in advance if you wish to conduct your meetings in English, but be prepared to accept a refusal—even if your counterpart speaks perfect English!

- It's advised that at least one member of your group speak Spanish. In addition to the respect it shows to your Mexican colleagues, it will help you understand the concerns of your Mexican counterparts better—during meetings conducted in English, they may talk extensively among themselves in Spanish. While speaking Spanish will win you friends, you should always be conscious of your limitations.

- English is widely understood and spoken by businesspeople and politicians. Tourist industry workers generally understand at least some English.

CORPORATE CULTURE:

Structure: The government is very active in the Mexican economy. Certain sectors of the economy have historically been under state control. Sectors of the economy either owned or dominated by the state include public utilities, petroleum, banking, basic manufacturing, mining, entertainment and many service industries. Privatization and liberalization are gradually but steadily underway and will probably accelerate under NAFTA.

Generally speaking, in Mexico power and authority rest with a person, as compared with the United States, where power and authority rest with a job title. For the most part, decisions in Mexico are centralized. The nature and type of decisions made are strongly influenced by the personality of the decision-maker.

Decisions in Mexico are centralized.

A great deal of foreign investment (primarily American, but also Japanese and English) has been made in the Mexican *maquiladoras,* assembly plants mostly located near the border with the United States that assemble foreign (mostly U.S.) manufactured components for re-export (mostly to the U.S.) and operate under special tax and export provisions.

The most common types of Mexican business entities are:

Mexican business entity–English equivalent

Sociedad Anónima (S.A.)–corporation

Sociedad Anónima de Capital Variable (S.A. de C.V.)–corporation with variable capital

Sociedad de Responsabilidad Limitada (S. en R.L.)–limited-liability company

Sociedad en Nombre Colectivo (S. en N.C.) – general partnership

Asociación en Participacion (A. en P.) – joint venture

Sociedad Civil (S.C.)–civil partnership (used by administrative service units and professional practitioners)

Asociación Civil (A.C.)–civil organization (used by charities and non-profits)

Meetings: Meet with top executives first. The Mexican group you meet with, at least initially, is normally determined as much by status as by competence with the particular matters to be discussed. Your group should include at least one high-ranking member of your company who has the power to make decisions. Top Mexican executives may absent themselves from subsequent meetings, which will take place with middle-level management and technical people. Don't feel insulted; this shows that discussions are proceeding positively.

Your host will direct you to your seat. Expect approximately ten to fifteen minutes of small talk to occur before getting down to business. This time is very important, and should be used to develop a personal relationship with your Mexican counterpart. If offered something to drink (usually coffee), don't refuse!—this would be seen as an insult.

Mexicans have different attitudes toward meetings than Americans and Canadians. Negotiations move slowly. Be patient. For Mexicans, the building of a personal relationship comes before the building of a professional relationship. Mexicans consider personal relationships more important than schedules. For Mexicans, lateness, changing topics and other concerns are a valid part of any meeting. Mexicans may feel constrained or inhibited by a tight schedule and may resent it.

Rule of Thumb

Be patient.

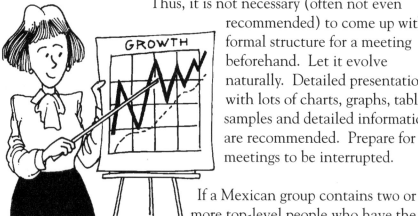

Thus, it is not necessary (often not even recommended) to come up with a formal structure for a meeting beforehand. Let it evolve naturally. Detailed presentations with lots of charts, graphs, tables, samples and detailed information are recommended. Prepare for meetings to be interrupted.

If a Mexican group contains two or more top-level people who have the same amount of authority, there may be some intra-group disagreements at the meeting. Make sure you know who holds the power to make decisions so as not to waste time with someone who can't affect the decision and who will ultimately accept whatever is decided. That's not to say, however, that those in positions of lesser authority are powerless. They can employ more indirect methods to influence their superior's decision if they are convinced that it is in their superior's best interest.

Make sure you know who has the power to make decisions.

Mexican and American or Canadian concepts of "order" are different. Mexicans have a more circular notion of order and will discuss more than one thing at a time (and may interrupt a meeting to attend to other matters). What Americans and Canadians view as intrusions (personal matters, other supposedly "unrelated" topics of conversation) are viewed as parts of a larger whole by Mexicans.

Take some time to consider before agreeing to anything—quick decisiveness is often seen as unduly hasty. Even when meetings get highly competitive, the competition will always be friendly and cordial.

Communication: Mexican communication is often marked by a flair for the dramatic. Elegance of expression and eloquence of language are particularly prized. Charisma may triumph over logic in communication. Always be warm and friendly when communicating with Mexicans. Don't be insincere, which can be easily detected. Little things such as warm hellos and good-byes and thank-you notes mean a lot.

Personal relationships and trust are very important and must be established before serious negotiations can ensue. A Mexican's impression of you as a person takes precedence over the status and power of your company. Don't talk about your company, talk about people.

Be prepared to talk about your personal life and to discuss personal beliefs and ideals when you want to discuss details and facts. View it like a courtship—making sure you're compatible before getting down to business.

Quick decisiveness is often seen as unduly hasty.

Personal relationships are very important and must be established before serious negotiations can ensue.

View business like a courtship.

Initial business communication styles in Mexico are more similar to those in Europe than those in the United States. Initial contacts are generally quite dignified and subdued. As relationships develop, communication styles may become somewhat more relaxed. Don't be offended by loud or boisterous displays later on—Mexicans can be quite demonstrative, but don't take it personally.

Faux Pas

Avoid asking direct questions or expressing strong disagreement.

Avoid asking direct questions or expressing strong disagreement. Mexican courtesy may result in foreign businesspeople being told what they want to hear. Flexibility is important. Listen closely and don't interrupt your Mexican counterpart. Always keep in mind that your responses should be calculated to present yourself as someone Mexicans can trust and respect and enjoy doing business with. Always show your counterparts the respect and deference they feel they are due.

You should always ask for written confirmation of any agreement or commitment. Courtesy may lead Mexicans to agree with you in person to avoid hurting your feelings or creating unpleasantness. Promises may be made as a show of strength and then not kept. For many Mexicans, to admit that they can't perform a certain action might be viewed as an admission of weakness. Thus, difficulties in implementing an agreed-upon plan often arise.

A promise does not mean that your request will be carried out. Mexicans tend to believe that the changeability of life can affect promises and deals in ways we can not predict. What can be said with certainty, however, is that if you are happy that a promise was made, then something good was accomplished.

Management or other important people may sometimes make unreasonable or overly aggressive demands in order to demonstrate their importance within or to their own group. Sometimes some Mexican men may act in ways that, by American or Canadian standards, seem too aggressive or power hungry, especially if they feel their manhood is being threatened or called into question. Be aware of such hidden agendas. If possible, discuss such matters in private with a Mexican with whom you have developed a good relationship to find out what he or she really needs. A good response to such actions would be to work toward your goal while showing the respect for your counterparts' power, thereby helping enhance his or her personal position in the eyes of his or her group.

Personalize everything! Explain how all proposals will benefit a Mexican's country, community, family, and most important, the Mexican personally. A logical analysis of how you (your product or project) can benefit your Mexican counterparts is certainly necessary for

Rule of Thumb

Personalize everything!

your business relationship. If a personal relationship isn't well-developed, however, such an analysis alone won't be enough. Personal relationships are more important than company relationships. For example, Lopez's firm, SA Internacional, does business with Johnson's firm, Amtech, because Lopez and Johnson have developed a good personal relationship.

"Macho" attitudes strongly influence communication, negotiating, and decision-making. Self-deprecating statements or jokes and modesty are not recommended behaviors for foreign men; they will be seen as signs of weakness.

Deal-making almost never occurs over the phone (and rarely by letter). Mexicans prefer to do business in person.

BE AWARE:

- With the implementation of NAFTA, visas are no longer required for business travelers to Mexico from the United States or Canada who plan to stay less than thirty-one days.

- An introduction by a respected third party is the best course. You may encounter some initial suspicion of your motives.

- Leave the lawyers at home during initial contacts. In Mexico, lawyers are often only introduced when difficulties arise or when a deal is about to be concluded.

- The Mexican concept of time is very different from that of an American or Canadian. Deadlines are often little more than (very) general target dates.

Deadlines are often little more than very general target dates.

- While the U.S.-Mexican relationship is improving rapidly, resentment still lingers about what the Mexicans consider bullying by their neighbor to the north. Never compare the way things are done in Mexico with the way they are done in the United States. A commitment to the long-term is viewed very positively. Historically, Mexicans have viewed their business dealings with Americans quite negatively; Americans are often seen as having stormed into Mexico, making a lot of money and then returning home.

Think long-term.

- A sense of fatalism or predestination may cause some Mexicans to take a more short-term approach to doing a business deal. They may work toward maximizing profits immediately while neglecting long-term planning. Some feel they are not creators of their path through life which is pre-ordained by God. Thus, an opportunity to make a lot of money in a short amount of time may be preferred, for tomorrow is impossible to predict.

- Your local contact person or representative is very important and should be chosen very carefully. A low-level representative will be taken as an affront by status-conscious Mexicans, who will assume that you are not really serious.

- The status of the hotel you stay at, the quality of your clothes and watch, whether or not you arrive in a chauffeured limousine or in a taxi, etc., will be critically appraised by your Mexican counterparts.

- Mexicans do not make large compromises, which they feel damage their integrity and honor. Therefore, do not exaggerate your initial proposal with the intention of later modifying it substantially. Of course some margin is necessary as leverage; while Mexicans do not like to compromise, they enjoy bargaining.

- There is a greater affinity between Mexicans and other Latin Americans than between Mexicans and Americans or Canadians. The actions of you, your company, and your country in another part of Latin America may influence the Mexican perception of you more than you realize.

- Be persistent! Don't give up if you don't receive a response to your phone calls or letters right away or if your meetings are continually postponed or canceled. If you give up, many Mexicans will assume that you weren't serious in the first place.

- Family ties are very important in Mexican business. Mexico is not a meritocracy—relationships, status and origins are more important than achievement.

- Upward mobility may be limited for your Mexican counterpart, especially at middle- and lower-management levels. Thus, a motivating factor is not a desire to get ahead (which they feel they can't), but rather to develop a good relationship so that they have your respect (and to demonstrate their respect for their boss).

- Personal initiative is not highly valued by most Mexicans, for they are more accustomed to authoritarian decision-making where explicit rules and guidelines are set down.

Rule of Thumb

Be persistent!

- Mexicans are uncomfortable with American or Canadian informality. Mexicans will not approach their superiors in an informal manner. If it is insisted that managers and workers interact with each other in a very informal manner, Mexican workers often try to avoid such interactions.

Mexicans are uncomfortable with American-style informality in business.

- Although the Mexican people are not at all happy with its continued existence, bribery (*la mordida*, literally "the bite") is unfortunately still prevalent in some areas of Mexico. Americans and Canadians are strongly advised not to engage in such illicit activities and should develop a firm, clear policy back home toward this practice before entering the Mexican market.

- Significant regional differences exist in the way business is conducted in Mexico. Regional rivalries and biases exist. Business is fast-paced and international in Mexico City, the political, commercial and cultural center of Mexico. Business in Monterrey tends to be conducted in a fast-paced and efficient manner like that in the United

Significant regional differences exist in the way business is conducted.

States, and the people of Monterrey like to assert their independence from the central government in Mexico City. The business culture in Guadalajara is much less international, centers more around particular families and tends to be more conservative and traditional.

ENTERTAINMENT:

- Business entertainment is very important! It is here that personal relationships should be developed. Expect to do much more business socializing in Mexico than is common in the United States.

Business entertaining is very important.

- Business is often discussed at meals. Business lunches are very common. They usually take place sometime after 2 p.m. and are the main meal of the day. Such lunches, however, are usually not all business, so relax and enjoy yourself—lunch can last for hours and sometimes end the business day!

Lunch can last for hours.

- Dinner is normally preceded by cocktails, with the meal starting between eight and nine. Dinner is usually a long, drawn-out affair. Discussions of family life and other personal matters generally occur at dinner. After you have finished eating, allow for continued conversation and discussion before calling the waiter.

- To reciprocate, invite your Mexican counterparts to dinner at a nice restaurant (French or Italian are your best bets). Pay in advance to avoid fights over the bill.

- Spouses are generally not included in business entertaining, at least initially. That said, spouses (and in Mexico this normally means wives) are certainly welcomed and are almost always included once the relationship (both professional and personal) moves beyond the initial stages.

- Businesspeople are often invited to visit the home of their Mexican counterparts.

APPOINTMENTS:

- Normal business hours are 9 a.m. to 6 p.m., Monday through Friday. Government offices are normally open from 9 a.m. to 2:30 p.m., banks from 9 a.m. to 1:30 p.m. Some banks in Mexico City stay open later and on Saturdays.

- Confirm your appointments about ten days before your meetings. Mexican businesspeople travel a lot, and sometimes appointments have to be rescheduled. Try to arrive at least one day early to make sure of your schedule.

- Morning appointments are best.

Morning appointments are best.

- Don't schedule visits to Mexico from December 16 to January 6, the week before Easter, and, if you are meeting with government officials, during elections.

- As elsewhere, the role and place of women in society is changing in Mexico. Historically, public life in Mexico has been a male-dominated domain, and very few women entered business or politics (and fewer held important positions). Increasingly, however, Mexican women—especially young, upper-class females—are active in business and as doctors, dentists, lawyers and teachers.

- Mexican men control Mexican society, and Mexican women control the men. Women have always been the dominant figures in Mexican private life. Traditionally, the Mexican father functions as the family spokesperson to the outside world while the mother rules family life.

- Mexican men are generally regarded as the most macho of all Latin Americans. Macho attitudes are more pronounced among the lower classes. Upper-class male machismo and attitudes toward women can be subtle. Talk and behavior considered sexist and inappropriate in the United

Mexican men control Mexican society. Mexican women control the men.

States may well have to be endured in Mexico.

- Women should prepare for some difficulty when doing business in Mexico. Because some Mexican businessmen you encounter may not have had many dealings with women in positions of authority in business, you should always immediately demonstrate to them your competence, skill and authority. Always be extremely professional, but don't overdo it (few things turn off Mexican men more than aggressive women).

- Mexican men, business colleagues included, will pay foreign businesswomen many compliments and may well flirt with you. While you may not be comfortable with this type of interplay between the sexes, it's part of the landscape in Mexico. Graciously accept and enjoy such banter— it is normally done with the utmost respect—while firmly reminding your male Mexican counterparts that you are a *business*woman (and never lead anyone on, unless you're prepared for the consequences).

- Foreign businesswomen should not invite Mexican businessmen to dinner unless their spouses also come along. If invited out to dinner or socializing by a male Mexican colleague, a businesswoman should make sure that he understands that no opportunity for romance exists. In Mexico, when a man and a women are alone, there is almost always the appearance or suspicion that a romance or a sexual relationship is developing (or has developed). Appearances are important!

- At business meals, a foreign businesswoman should arrange payment with the restaurant beforehand. If not, the Mexican businessman will feel obliged to pay and will be insulted if not allowed to.

- A woman sitting alone in a bar in Mexico is thought by most Mexican males to be looking for companionship. If you really feel like a drink, the hotel bar is your best bet.

- Generally speaking, foreign women won't encounter considerably more harassment in large Mexican cities than they would in other North American and European cities of a commensurate size. Outside major cities, however, it's a different story. Advances and harassment can be quite brazen in these areas; it is advised to bring along a friend or colleague when you go out in public.

Rule of Thumb

Foreign businesswomen should not invite Mexican businessmen to dinner unless their spouses come along.

- By American and Canadian standards, Mexican women are very made-up. Mexicans often see American and Canadian women as not feminine enough, and act negatively when they encounter women who "act like men."

HEALTH AND SAFETY

*Make sure your
insurance covers
you in Mexico.*

*Travelers to all
coastal areas
should always use
insect repellent.*

Medical facilities in Mexico differ from those in the United States. Treatment for some types of illnesses or injuries may be only remedial. Some remote areas and coastal islands have few or no medical facilities. Make sure that your medical insurance covers you while in Mexico. If not, it is advised to take out a short-term supplemental policy. If you will be in remote areas, supplemental medical evacuation assistance is also advised.

Immunizations against diphtheria, tetanus, polio, typhoid, and hepatitis A are recommended. If you are traveling to an area known to be infected with yellow fever, a vaccination certificate is required. Malaria is found in some rural areas of Mexico, particularly those near the southwest coast. If you intend to be in these areas, consult your physician and take the recommended dosage of chloroquine. Travelers to all coastal areas should always use insect repellent and take precautions to minimize contact with mosquitoes, particularly from dusk to dawn when malaria transmission is most likely.

Drink only bottled water or water that has been boiled for twenty minutes. Avoid ice cubes. If you can't peel it or have it safely cooked, don't eat it. "Montezuma's revenge" is no myth. Diarrhea is potentially dangerous—if symptoms persist, seek medical assistance.

Altitude sickness may affect those in Mexico City. Symptoms include lack of energy, a tendency to tire easily, shortness of breath, occasional dizziness, and insomnia. You may need a short adjustment period. Minimize your consumption of alcohol. Take very special care if you decide to work out at high altitudes. Air pollution in Mexico City is severe and peaks during dangerous inversions that most often occur from December to May. The elderly and those who have high blood pressure, anemia, or respiratory or cardiac problems should consult their doctor before traveling to Mexico City.

Beware of pickpockets and purse-snatchers. Walk at a distance from the curb to avoid thieves on motorcycles. As in the U.S., always avoid dark alleys and marginal areas, and be very careful in crowds. Mexican drug laws are extremely strict. Public drunkenness is against the law. It is not wise to carry anything that might be construed as a weapon; many areas

Rule of Thumb

Drink only bottled water or water that has been boiled for twenty minutes.

have strict laws banning such items. Driving in Mexico is not for the faint of heart and is not recommended for visitors. If you decide to drive in Mexico, consult AAA or a travel agency for rules and guidelines.

STOP AND GO

Cultural differences can cause misunderstandings even when you think you understand everything perfectly. On my first visit to Mexico, I was confused by the traffic signs. I knew that the international traffic symbol for "stop" is an octagon, and I was pretty sure that the Spanish word for "stop" is alto, *but, after my driver sped through sign after sign with nary a pause, I started to have my doubts. I decided to ask my driver, and he quickly responded, "Well, technically, yes,* alto *does means "stop" in Spanish, but in Mexican it means "slow down a little."*

EMERGENCY NUMBERS:

Dial 06 for local police assistance.

The Mexican Ministry of Tourism staffs a 24-hour hotline to assist tourists in an emergency: [91] (5) 250-0123. The first number [91] is the long-distance access code, the second number (5) is the city code and the last number is the local phone number.

You can also call the Silver Angels, a special group that helps foreigners who are victims of

crime to file a police report. Their number is
[91] (5) 588-5100.

The number for the United States Embassy in
Mexico City is (5) 211-0042.

January:	St. Anthony's Day (17).	
February:	Carnival (week before Lent).	
March:	Birthday of Benito Juárez (21).	
March/April:	Easter.	
May:	Labor Day (1), Cinco de Mayo (5).	
May/June:	Corpus Christi.	
August:	Assumption (15).	
September:	Independence Day (16).	
October:	Columbus Day (12).	
November:	All Saints Day (1), All Souls Day (2), Revolution Day (20).	
December:	Day of the Virgin of Guadalupe (12), Christmas (25).	

HOLIDAYS AND FESTIVALS

NOTE: Official holidays fall on the same date
every year (even when they occur on a

Sunday). Many Catholic holidays are celebrated in Mexico, but are not official holidays.

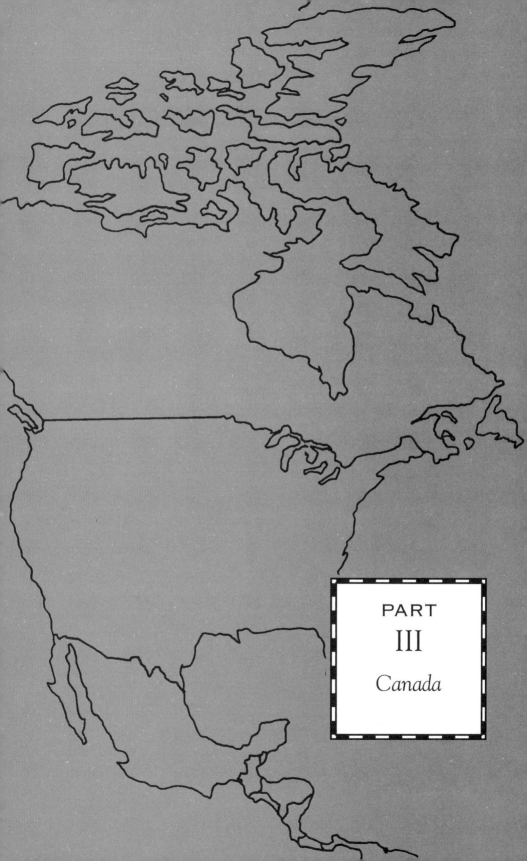

PART
III

Canada

N

YUKON

NORTHWEST TERRITORIES

BRITISH COLUMBIA

ALBERTA

Edmonton

Calgary

Vancouver

SASKATCHEWAN

MANITOBA

ONTARIO

QUEBEC

NEWFOUNDLAND

Montreal

OTTAWA

Toronto

PRINCE EDWARD ISLAND

NOVA SCOTIA

NEW BRUNSWICK

UNITED STATES

The boundaries and city locations of this map are not intended to be geographically accurate.

Veves Castle, Veves, Belgium

Five continents, One carrier...

Roadway Express now offers international door-to-door service to over fifty-five countries on five continents. With service through all major ports, you get the benefits of a single carrier, computerized tracking and only one invoice. So if you're thinking of shipping internationally, call your local Roadway representative or call our International Hotline at **1-800-INTL-REX**.

ROADWAY®

Working Expressly For You

21.
LETTER FROM CANADA

Just as I've done with Mexico, I've asked my Canadian friends how they view Americans and what points they'd like to make to Americans who visit Canada. Here is a compilation of some of their more interesting and relevant comments:

Dear American Friends,

You asked what we Canadians think about you Americans. Honestly, we like America and Americans. We admire many things about you. You are outgoing, friendly, generous, independent, and filled with an optimism and "can-do" spirit like no other people in the world. On the whole, we find Americans to be delightful, intelligent, charming people.

There is no denying that the United States is a central presence in Canadian life and politics. Although we sometimes may not like to admit it, we Canadians constantly look at the United States as a point of reference. We are a middle power sharing the continent with a superpower. While the United States exerts a great deal of influence over events in Canada, the reverse is not true. The American media is prevalent in Canada, and American pop culture is pervasive (many contributors to "American" pop culture, however—from anchorman Peter Jennings to actors William Shatner, Michael J. Fox and Donald Sutherland, to name but a handful—are in fact Canadians).

Our countries remain the firmest of allies, our peoples the best of friends. We are each others' number one trading partners. 20 per cent of all U.S. exports go to Canada (the United States exports more to Ontario alone than to all of Japan!). It will probably surprise you to learn that we Canadians invest as much in the United States as Americans do in Canada. 45 percent of all tourists to the United States come from Canada. So many of us—especially from Quebec—spend the winter in the greater Miami area that Florida has been jokingly called "Canada's 11th province."

Canadians invest as much in the United States as Americans do in Canada.

Our occasional differences are thought of as "in the family," and we can usually work out a mutually acceptable resolution.

We must admit to a certain ambivalence, however, for while we like Americans, we don't want to be like Americans. While the major strength of the U.S.-Canadian relationship is that our two countries are so similar, it is perhaps also the major weakness. Perhaps it is because we are so alike in many ways that we Canadians spend so much time looking for differences between our countries and peoples. But the differences are important.

It seems to us that Americans are not sensitive to many of the important differences between our countries. You assume that Canada and Canadians are no different from the United States and Americans. A famous historian has stated that "Americans are benevolently ignorant about Canada, while Canadians are malevolently well-informed about the United States." Only we don't find your ignorance so benevolent. To us, it seems arrogant. While Canadians are very aware of contemporary American culture and politics, the reverse is not true. We take courses in American history in school; in a recent survey more than half of you couldn't even name the capital of our country.

It may come as a surprise to you that we have different views on the history we "share" with the United States. Our two countries emerged from the American War for Independence, and have been on parallel but different cultural and historical tracks. While we decided to retain our ties to Britain, your country was born of "revolution." Many of the early Canadians were Loyalists to the British crown who came fleeing the discord in the Colonies.

While the major strength of the U.S.-Canadian relationship is that our two countries are so similar, it is perhaps also the major weakness.

Our countries have been on parallel but different cultural and historical tracks.

Compared with the United States, we Canadians place a greater value on collective (as opposed to individual) rights. Our government is more involved in our economy and culture. Canada is not as litigious a society as the United States; we work almost instinctively toward mediation and negotiation and away from confrontation. We tend to be more reserved than Americans. Your aggressiveness and habit for labeling everything the "biggest," "best," "fastest" or "richest" (the "-est syndrome") sometimes irritates us.

Canada is home to a great variety of geography, peoples and cultures. Although historically of predominantly European heritage, more and more Canadians trace their roots back to places like the Indian subcontinent, East Asia and Africa. You famously describe your country as a "melting pot"; we Canadians like to think of our country as a "multicultural mosaic," where many different cultural and ethnic groups join together while working to maintain their unique identities.

We Canadians like to think of our country as a "multicultural mosaic."

Important regional differences exist in Canada. From the stable and more traditional provinces of the East to Quebec, a mostly French-speaking society and the most notably unique region in Canada, through Ontario to the prairie states and on to British Columbia,

Canada's "tomorrowland," each area is distinctly different. Many Canadians identify strongly with their particular area of the country.

Our countries share the longest undefended border in the world. When you cross this border, please remember that you are in another country, with different laws, cultures, mores, and norms.

Take the time to learn about Canada. Read a Canadian newspaper or magazine. Enjoy a novel by a Canadian writer like Margaret Atwood, Robertson Davies or Sinclair Ross. Tune your radio in to the CBC, our excellent national broadcast system. Explore our country's vast natural beauty. Spend some time wandering the streets of our modern, safe cities. But most of all, take the time to get to know us personally.

We're proud of our country, our homes, cultures and traditions, and would like them respected.

Please come visit us, but come informed and with an open mind.

Sincerely,

Your Canadian Friends

Our countries share the longest undefended border in the world.

22.

THE TEN COMMANDMENTS OF DOING BUSINESS IN CANADA

1. Do your homework! A basic knowledge of Canadian culture and history will be richly rewarded.

2. Ask, look and listen! A respectful interest in Canadian culture will be appreciated.

3. Try! It is better to try and make a mistake than not to try at all.

4. When a problem develops, assume miscommunication was the cause.

5. Recognize and acknowledge the uniqueness of Canada and Canadians. Never regard Canada as a mere appendage to the United States.

6. Don't treat Canada as an extension of the U.S. market.

7. Tailor your marketing effort to the specific region of Canada you wish to enter. Use French in your marketing effort in Quebec.

8. Be aware of special laws regarding the use of English and French.

9. Be sincere. Sincerity shows, and is required to build trust. Trust is required to build a relationship.

10. Hire a reliable team of experts to take you into the Canadian market.

23.
CANADA

VITAL STATISTICS

POPULATION: 28 million (1994). Approximately four-fifths live within 100 miles of the border with the United States (populated Canada has been likened to a "horizontal Chile" sandwiched between the tundra and the forty-ninth parallel). 80 percent urban, but has a very small overall population density of 7 per square mile (lower than North Dakota). The greatest population density is found in the so-called Golden Triangle in southern Ontario and southern Quebec. No permanent settlements are found on 89 percent of Canadian soil.

CAPITAL: Ottawa (metropolitan population, including Hull: 920,000).

MAJOR CITIES: Montreal (3 million), Toronto (3.5 million), Vancouver (1.6 million), Edmonton (840,000), Calgary (754,000).

LAND AREA:	3,849,674 square miles. The second largest country in the world after Russia, Canada is nearly as big as all of Europe and spans six (and a half) time zones.
GOVERNMENT:	Federation of ten provinces and two territories. Democratic parliamentary monarchy. The prime minister is the head of government and is chosen by the majority party in the House of Commons. The Queen of England is officially the head of state; she appoints a governor-general to represent her in Canada. Two-house parliament consists of a 104-member Senate (appointed by the governor-general) and a popularly elected 295-member House of Commons.
PROVINCES (CAPITALS):	Alberta (Edmonton), British Columbia (Victoria), Manitoba (Winnipeg), New Brunswick (Fredericton), Newfoundland (St. John's), Northwest Territories (Yellowknife), Nova Scotia (Halifax), Ontario (Toronto), Prince Edward Island (Charlottetown), Quebec (Quebec City), Saskatchewan (Regina), Yukon Territory (Whitehorse).
LIVING STANDARD:	GDP = $US19,650 (1993).
NATURAL RESOURCES:	Canada is blessed with an abundance of natural resources. Timber, fish (cod, lobster, salmon), petroleum, natural gas, nickel, copper, gold, zinc,

coal, iron ore, aluminum. 30 percent of the world's fresh water.

AGRICULTURE: Beef cattle, milk, wheat, hogs, chickens, canola, eggs.

INDUSTRY: Motor vehicles, mining and ore processing, food products, paper products, wood products, chemicals, electronic equipment, printed materials, machinery.

CLIMATE: Few general observations can be made about the climate of a country as vast as Canada. Temperatures in the middle of the country are characterized by extremes, with long, cold winters and hot summers. The weather on the coasts is more moderate. Above the Arctic circle, it is so cold in many places that the minus is omitted from temperature readings for much of the year.

CURRENCY: Dollar. Paper bills come in denominations of 100, 20, 10, 5 and 2 dollars, coins in denominations of 1 dollar (affectionately called a "loony"), 25, 10, 5 and 1 cent(s). Bills in 1 dollar denominations have been discontinued, although some still remain in circulation.

THE PEOPLE

CORRECT NAME: Canadians, *Les Canadiens*

ETHNIC MAKEUP: The vast majority of Canadians claim European ancestry. Four in nine Canadians claim some British ancestry, a little less than one in three Canadians have some French ancestry. 80 percent of those in Quebec have French ancestry. 80 percent of native French speakers live in Quebec (the others are mostly in New Brunswick, and parts of Ontario and Manitoba). Other European groups include Italians, Germans and Ukrainians (especially in the prairie provinces).

Many people (especially from the Indian subcontinent and the Caribbean) have migrated from within the Commonwealth to Canada. Large numbers of Hong Kong Chinese have settled in the Vancouver area in anticipation of the return of Hong Kong to China in 1997. Small numbers of Inuits, Métis, and Amerindians (called "People of the First Nations"). About 1 percent Black (predominantly from the Caribbean).

Canadians think of their country as a "multi-cultural mosaic," and not a "melting pot." Federal policies encourage the maintenance of distinct cultural groupings.

Although the use of such terms has persisted in some quarters, members of different ethnic groups are not widely known as "hyphenated" Canadians (i.e. not African-Canadians or Chinese-Canadians). They are all Canadians. Recent arrivals to Canada are known as "New Canadians." Canada doesn't keep criminal statistics based on race.

VALUE SYSTEM/
NATIONAL TRAITS: Canadians are very friendly, open, courteous and not dogmatic. They are individualistic and materialistic, although not to the extent of their neighbors to the south. Canadians are generally more formal than Americans, more casual than Europeans. Canadian society is egalitarian and democratic.

Broadly speaking, Canada has been divided into two distinct societies, one French-speaking (see "Regional Differences" below) and one English-speaking. Because they don't form as cohesive a group as French-speaking Canadians, only very general observations can be made about English-speaking Canadians; they are generally thought of (and consider themselves) more reserved, less aggressive and less excitable than their neighbors to the south.

Most Canadians identify themselves very strongly with their province. Canadians continue to wrestle with the question, "What does it mean to be Canadian?" and take pains to differentiate themselves from citizens of the United States.

The Canadian constitution guarantees "peace, order and good government" (contrast with "life, liberty and the pursuit of happiness" from the American Declaration of Independence.) and Canadians like to consider themselves good citizens. Canadians take pride in their low crime rate. The oft-cited Canadian deference to authority (the Royal Canadian Mounted Police, or "Mounties" and the Queen, for example) is somewhat overblown.

REGIONAL
DIFFERENCES:

Atlantic Canada (includes the Maritimes—Nova Scotia, New Brunswick, and Prince Edward Island—and Newfoundland): Primarily of British descent, the residents of the less prosperous Atlantic provinces are generally more reserved, stolid, provincial and old-fashioned. Newfoundland is unique, with a dialect and culture that draws comparisons with the Irish and the people of western England.

Ontario: Residents of Canada's most populous province—the country's economic, political and cultural colossus—are generally thought of as more business-like and conservative than other Canadians.

Western Canada (includes Alberta, Saskatchewan and Manitoba): Residents of Canada's western provinces are generally more open, relaxed, friendly and direct than other Canadians (comparisons are often made with inhabitants of the midwestern and western United States).

British Columbia: Canada's unconventional westernmost province is seen by Canadians as the land of the future, and has more in common with Seattle than Toronto. Like many other western Canadians, many residents of B.C. feel somewhat estranged from "Easterners" (a general code word for those from Ontario and Quebec).

Quebec (and other areas of French-speaking Canada): Québécois (or citizens of Quebec, pronounced "keh-beck-wah") have a very strong sense of cultural identity and are very nationalistic. The European influence is strongly felt in Quebec, whose people consider themselves the "defenders of French civilization in North America." Due to their animated good nature, Québécois are sometimes called the "Latins of the North."

The North: Residents of the sparsely populated north are seen as rugged embodiments of Canadian pioneer spirit.

FAMILY:	Small family size, low divorce rate. Both parents usually work outside the home. Living together before marriage is common, especially in urban areas.
RELIGION:	Generally speaking, most Québécois (as well as French-speaking Canadians living outside of Quebec) are Roman Catholic, and most other Canadians are Protestant (primarily Anglican, Presbyterian and United Church). Small numbers of Jews, Muslims, Buddhists, Hindus, and Sikhs. Official separation of church and state, but religious organizations are more actively involved in education and politics than in the United States.
EDUCATION:	Responsibility for schooling is left to the individual provinces, and significant variations occur. The state provides funding for schools run by religious organizations. Except for native English-speakers who move to Quebec and at a few universities, all schooling in Quebec is in French. 99 percent literacy.
SPORTS:	Ice hockey, baseball, Canadian football, lacrosse, soccer, skating, skiing, curling.

IMPORTANT DATES

1534	Jacques Cartier arrives in North America and claims the area for France.
1756	The Seven Years War (also known in North America as the French and Indian War) breaks out between England and France. Fighting over possessions in North America ensues.
1763	Treaty of Paris grants the areas of New France to the British.
1812	Toronto is sacked during the War of 1812, the last armed conflict between the United States and Canada (part of Great Britain). Hostilities end in 1814.
1842	Upper Canada (Ontario) and Lower Canada (Quebec) united.
1867	British North America Act proclaims the Dominion of Canada. Sir John A. Macdonald becomes prime minister, a position he holds (with one five-year break) until 1891.
1914-18	Canadians fight in World War I.
1921	W. L. Mackenzie King elected prime minister, serves with two interruptions (1926, 1930-1935) until 1948.
1931	The Statute of Westminster formally grants Canada foreign policy independence from Great Britain.
1939-45	Canadian troops fight in World War II.
1949	Newfoundland becomes a province of Canada.

1950-53	Canadian troops fight in the Korean War as part of the United Nations forces.
1960s	The "Quiet Revolution" brings increased attention to the rights and aspirations of French-speaking Canadians.
1967	Montreal hosts the World's Fair.
1968	Pierre Trudeau becomes Prime Minster, serving (with a short interruption in 1979-1980) until 1984.
1969	Official Languages Act requires that federal services be given in English and French if 10 percent of a particular population speak either language.
1970	Separatist terrorists kidnap a Quebec cabinet minister (later executed) and a British diplomat (later released), leading to imposition of the War Measures Act.
1976	The separatist Parti Québécois (PQ), led by René Lévesque, wins provincial elections in Quebec.
1977	Bill 101 makes French the official language of Quebec.
1980	Referendum on separation defeated by Quebec voters.
1984	Brian Mulroney replaces Trudeau as prime minister, serving until 1993.
1988	Calgary hosts the Winter Olympics.
1989	U.S.-Canadian Free Trade Agreement (CFTA) implemented, starts process (among other things) of the elimination of all tariffs within ten years between the two countries.

1990	A constitutional amendment—known as the Meech Lake Accord—recognizing Quebec as a distinct society fails to pass in two provincial legislatures, and does not become law.
1993	Kim Campbell serves a short term as Canada's first female prime minister. Jean Chrétien elected Prime Minister.
1994	North American Free Trade Agreement (NAFTA) goes into effect, linking the economies of Canada, the United States and Mexico.

MEETING AND GREETING

- In general, Canadians are more reserved and polite than Americans and take matters of etiquette a little more seriously.

- Shake hands and introduce yourself when meeting Canadians for the first time. Always shake hands firmly when meeting or departing. Eye contact is important.

- When a woman enters or leaves a room, it is polite for men to rise. Men normally offer their hand to a woman.

- In Quebec, kissing on the cheeks in the French manner is quite common. When close friends and family meet in Quebec, they use first names and kiss both cheeks.

- An older Québécois man may kiss the hand of a woman. Accept this gesture graciously. A foreign man shouldn't kiss the hand of a Québécois woman, who would be quite shocked.

NAMES AND TITLES

- Although the practice varies widely, Canadians in general are somewhat more formal than Americans with regard to names and titles. Use last names and appropriate titles until invited by your Canadian hosts or colleagues to use their first names. Western Canadians may use first names more quickly than other Canadians.

- The female titles Ms., Miss, and Mrs. are used as in the United States (although political correctness hasn't—yet—had the same impact in Canada as in the United States).

- Canadians normally address medical doctors as "doctor"; Ph.D.s are normally not addressed as "doctor," except sometimes in academia.

QUEBEC:

- Coworkers of similar status generally use first names in private but always last names in public. The formal "you" (*vous*) is almost always used in a business setting. Allow the older person to suggest the use of *tu*–the informal "you."

- Address people as *Monsieur, Madame* or *Mademoiselle* without adding the surname.

Mr.	*Monsieur*	mih-syoor
Mrs.	*Madame*	mah-dahm
Miss	*Mademoiselle*	mahd-mwah-zehl

Madame is used for all adult women, married or single, over 18 years of age (except for waitresses, whom you should address as *Mademoiselle*).

- Academic titles and degrees are important. When dealing with Québécois, you should know and use them properly.

Examples:

University professor	*Monsieur le professeur / Madame la professeur*
Lawyer	*Maître*
Ph.D.	*Monsieur le Docteur / Madame la Docteur*
M.D.	*Docteur*

LANGUAGE

- Canada has two official languages: English and French (since the Official Languages Act of 1969). French is the official language of Quebec; New Brunswick and the federal district of Ottawa are officially bilingual. In all other provinces, English is the official language. Many immigrants, Inuit and Amerindians continue to use their native languages.

English is the primary language of about two-thirds of all Canadians; French is the native tongue of a little more than one-fifth of all Canadians.

- English is the primary language of a little more than two-thirds of all Canadians, French of a little more than one-fifth of all Canadians.

- 80 percent of Canadian French speakers live in Quebec.

- In 1977, the passage of Bill 101, the Charter of the French language, made French the official language—of government, education and commerce—of Quebec. In 1989, after much contentious debate over the banning of English on publicly displayed signs in 1985, Quebec law was amended to allow languages other than French to be displayed on French-language signs as long as the French is "markedly predominant" and "deemed to have a greater visual impact."

- Canadian English is somewhat different from American English. People from outside North America find the standard American and Canadian accents nearly indistinguishable. Many British pronunciations (for example again is "uh-GAIN," been is "bean," schedule is "SHED-jual,") and spellings are employed (although many newspapers now use American spellings). American slang is common.

Canadian English is somewhat different from American English.

- Anglophone Canadians generally use the British pronunciation of the letter z ("zed"), although the American "zee" is becoming more common.

- An "eh," occasionally appended to the end of a statement or question (but very unlikely to be used in a business setting), is a trademark of the Canadian vernacular.

Don't mock this or attempt to mimic the Canadian accent.

- The working class dialect of French spoken in Canada (*joual*) is unique to Quebec. Looked down on by many Québécois, *joual* is characterized by elided syllables, English words conjugated according to French rules, and words unique to Quebec. Many French have difficulty understanding it—some films done in the Quebec dialect have been dubbed in France!

- In Montreal, you may hear conversations in a mixture of French and English.

- Outside of Quebec, French is spoken by small numbers of Canadians in New Brunswick, Ontario and Manitoba. In Western Canada, very few people speak French well.

STOP

A good example of the contention and passions aroused by the language question in Canada is the debate over how to label stop signs in Quebec. Many Quebec nationalists objected to the English word "stop" prominently displayed on red octagonal signs at intersections in the province. The search for the appropriate French-language equivalent, however, turned out to be more difficult than anticipated. The correct word in French is halte *(for what it's worth, "stop" is used in France), but* halte *is not used in joual. The authorities were left with one alternative: While perhaps not technically correct,* arrêt *now graces all stop signs in Canada's French-speaking province.*

- Generally speaking, Canadians are more reserved than Americans. Canadians generally don't touch very much when conversing. Maintaining a certain amount of personal space is important.

- Québécois are generally more animated and expressive than other Canadians.

- Take off your hat or sunglasses when speaking with someone.

- Canadians share many common gestures with Americans.

- Be aware that some gestures have different meanings in Quebec. For example, "thumbs down" is considered offensive in Quebec, as is slapping an open palm over a closed fist. Like the rest of their countrymen and -women, Québécois use the "thumbs up" sign to mean "okay." The "okay" sign made with the index finger and thumb means "zero" in Quebec.

- Sneeze or blow your nose as quietly as possible using a handkerchief or tissue. If

BODY LANGUAGE

Québécois are generally more animated and expressive than other Canadians.

possible, leave the room. Do not yawn or scratch in public. Toothpicks, nail clippers, and combs are never used in public. It's considered bad form to talk with your hands in your pockets. Don't sit with your legs apart or your feet propped up on a table or chair.

FRENCH PHRASES:

English	French	Pronunciation
Good morning/day/ afternoon	Bonjour	bohn-ZHOOR
Good evening	*Bon soir*	bohn-SWAHR
Please	*S'il vous plait*	seel voo PLEH
Thank you	*Merci*	mehr-SEE
You're welcome	*De rien*	deh ree-EHN
Yes	*Oui*	wee
No	*Non*	noh
Excuse me	*Pardon* *Excusez-moi*	pahr-DOHN ehk-skoo-zay-MWAH
Good-bye	*Au revoir*	o reh-VWAHR
How are you?	*Comment allez-vous?*	koh-mohn-tah-lay-VOO
Pleased to meet you	*Enchanté*	ahn-shahn-TAY

MANNERS

Etiquette and formalities are more important in Canada than in the United States.

DINING

The chic way to beckon a waiter in Quebec is to say *Monsieur* or *S'il vous plaît* rather than the traditional French *Garçon*. Say *Mademoiselle* to beckon a waitress. Never beckon a waiter or waitress by snapping your fingers or shouting.

- Etiquette and formalities are more important in Canada than in the United States.

- While the continental style (fork remains in the left hand) is employed when eating, the American style (i.e. the fork is switched back and forth between the hands) is sometimes used. Most Québécois eat in the continental style.

- In Quebec, keep your hands above the table when eating. The approach to food in Quebec is similar to that in France.

- Eating while walking or standing on the street in Quebec is considered bad form.

DRINKING AND TOASTING:

- Drinking and toasting habits among Anglophone Canadians are similar to those in the United States. "Cheers" is an acceptable toast.

- The most common toast in Quebec, used at both formal and informal occasions, is *a votre sante* (or "to your health," pronounced ah voh-TRAH sahn-TAY). The host normally offers the first toast. Wait until everyone is served wine and a toast is proposed before drinking. It is acceptable for a woman to propose a toast.

- The midday meal in Quebec follows French custom and can take up to two hours. Wine is normally served with meals in Quebec.

TIPPING:

- Tipping practices in Canada are similar to those in the United States.

- In restaurants, a service charge of 10-15 percent is usually included in the bill (*service compris* in French). Small change can be left on the table as an additional gratuity for good service. If the service charge is not included (*service non compris*), leave a 10-15 percent tip. Note that federal and provincial taxes (GST/PST) will also be in the bill.

DRESS

- Generally speaking, Canadians dress more conservatively (and more formally when going out) than their American neighbors, although practices vary by region. Dress in Vancouver, for example, is somewhat more casual, in Toronto more British. Québécois

Bring a sweater along, no matter what time of year you travel to Canada.

dress in a more relaxed, fashionable, European style than their fellow Canadians.

• It's a good idea to bring a sweater along, no matter what time of year you travel to Canada.

BUSINESS:

• Men: Suit and tie.

• Women: Conservative business outfit.

• The practice of having a "casual day" at the office (usually Friday) is becoming more common in Canada.

RESTAURANT:

• Generally speaking, Canadians dress more formally than Americans when eating out.

• Men: Coat and tie.

• Women: Dress or nice pants.

HOSTESS:

- You should bring flowers, fine wine or chocolates for the hostess when visiting a Canadian home. Avoid red roses (associated with romantic love) and white lilies (associated with funerals).

BUSINESS:

- The protocol for giving and receiving business gifts in Canada is similar to that in the United States. Generally, business gifts in Canada tend to be small and conservative.

GIFTS

DO:

- Do your homework about Canada. Most Americans are appallingly ignorant of Canadian history, culture and geography.

- Recognize that Canada is the most important trading partner of the United States.

- Recognize that important regional differences exist in Canada and prepare to adapt.

- Pay for goods and services in Canadian dollars. While U.S. dollars are widely (although sometimes rather begrudgingly)

HELPFUL HINTS

Most Americans are appallingly ignorant of Canadian history, culture and geography.

Important regional differences exist in Canada.

accepted at shops and restaurants all over Canada, the rate of exchange is normally very unfavorable. Change your money at a bank.

- When in Quebec, learn a little French; Québécois greatly appreciate it when you make the effort to talk to them in their native language.

- Canada uses the metric system. If you plan to drive in Canada, you should know that one U.S. gallon equals 3.78 liters; one Canadian imperial gallon equals 4.5 liters. To convert Celsius temperatures to Fahrenheit, multiply by 9, divide by 5 and add 32 (or if you just want an approximation, multiply by 2 and add 32).

- Canada has a federal Goods and Services Tax (GST), which operates similarly to the European VAT. Also, many provinces add on an additional Provincial Sales Tax (PST). Ask about refund policies, and keep your receipts!

DO NOT:

- Do not compare Canada with the United States.

- Although this should hardly need mentioning, do not view Canada as merely an extension of the United States.

- Do not use the term "Native Americans" to refer to indigenous peoples. Many Canadians find the use of the term offensive. Canadians refer to a member of one of these groups as "someone from the First Nations," or sometimes as native Canadians or aboriginals.

- Never sing "Alouette" to Québécois, which they find very condescending.

- Do not take sides in debates about contentious national issues (especially when they concern such issues as the status of Quebec, the place of the French and English languages in Canadian society, etc.).

Do not take sides in debates about contentious national issues.

PUNCTUALITY

- Punctuality is demanded for business meetings and social occasions. That said, Canadians are not as obsessed with time as Americans.

Punctuality is demanded for business and social occasions.

- Never arrive early for a social occasion. As in the United States, "fashionably late" is acceptable in Canada. Showing up early at a bar or disco in Quebec (at, say, ten o'clock) immediately marks you as an "Anglo."

STRICTLY BUSINESS

BUSINESS CARDS:

- Business cards are commonly exchanged in Canada.

- In Quebec, use business cards printed in English or French, including any academic degrees and titles. A double-sided business card (one side in English, one side in French) is best.

LANGUAGE:

- English and French are the official languages of business in Canada. Virtually all international business is conducted in English. French is the official language of the province of Quebec.

- Most Québécois speak and understand English, but prefer to use French. An interpreter will most likely not be necessary, but check ahead of time.

CORPORATE CULTURE:

- Generally speaking, business culture in Canada is quite similar to that in the United States, but a little more formal.

- Business culture in Quebec shows a French influence.

Structure: Government plays a much greater role in the Canadian economy than it does in the United States.

The corporation is the most common business entity in Canada. Canadian corporations may be incorporated under either federal or provincial law, and private corporations are much more common than they are in the United States.

Meetings: Canadians get down to business quickly. Meetings are well-organized, and extraneous discussion is kept to a minimum. A premium is placed on time.

Communication: English is the language of international business in Canada. Special laws exist in Quebec regarding the use of languages other than French. As in the United States, business communication in Canada is normally rather direct, although perhaps somewhat more reserved than in the United States. Many Canadians dislike the American hard-sell approach. Letters and telephone calls should be direct and succinct. Pleasantries are dispensed with very quickly. In some areas of Canada, businesspeople do not immediately call each other by their first names. Business relationships are somewhat more proper and formal than in the United States.

BE AWARE:

- Business culture varies somewhat throughout Canada, depending on the region.

- Although the relationship between Canada and the United States is generally quite good, some Canadians may be wary about the intentions of American businesses and put off by what they perceive as American arrogance.

ENTERTAINMENT:

- Business entertainment is common, but the focus usually remains on business.

- Business meals are very common. The person who invites is normally expected to pay.

APPOINTMENTS:

- Time is very valuable to Canadians, and punctuality is demanded. If a conflict arises, you are expected to let your Canadian counterpart know immediately.

- Normal business hours are 9 a.m. to 5 p.m., Monday through Friday. Store hours vary somewhat between provinces.

- Women are accepted and well-represented in business in Canada.

- A businesswoman can invite a Canadian businessman to lunch or dinner with no problem; the person who invites normally pays.

- In 1993, Kim Campbell became the first female prime minister of Canada. The current deputy prime minister is Sheila Copps.

- In Quebec, women should dress well but conservatively for business meetings.

- It is unlawful to carry Mace in Canada.

Women are accepted and well-represented in business in Canada.

HEALTH AND SAFETY

The United Nations has determined that Canada has the highest human development index (which measures such things as life expectancy, adult literacy, real per capita GDP, etc.) in the world. The Canadian health care system is among the best in the world. No special medical precautions are required for entry into Canada. The water is fine.

Canadians take justifiable pride in their low crime rate. Many Americans are amazed

The United Nations has determined that Canada has the highest human development index in the world.

at Canadians' ability to walk safely through their cities after dark.

EMERGENCY NUMBERS:
Throughout Canada, dial 911 or 0.

HOLIDAYS AND FESTIVALS		
January:	New Year's (1).	
February:	Carnival de Québec (in Quebec).	
March/April:	Good Friday, Easter Monday.	
May:	Victoria Day (Anglo-Canada) (third Monday), Dollard des Ormeaux (Quebec) (third Monday).	
June:	St. Jean Baptiste Day (the provincial holiday of Quebec, also known as *Fête Nationale*) (24).	
July:	Canada Day (1).	
August:	Civic holiday* (first Monday).	
September:	Labour Day (first Monday).	
October:	Thanksgiving (second Monday).	
November:	Remembrance Day (11).	

DECEMBER: Christmas (25),
              Boxing Day (26).

*August second is celebrated as Heritage Day
in Alberta, British Columbia Day in British
Columbia, and as a civic holiday in Manitoba,
New Brunswick, the New Territories, Ontario
and Saskatchewan.

The following provincial holidays are usually
celebrated in Newfoundland on the Monday
nearest the anniversary date: Commonwealth
Day (second Monday in March), St. Patrick's
Day (March 17), St. George's Day (April 23),
Discovery Day (June 27), Memorial Day (July
7) and Orangeman's Day (July 10).

Discovery Day is celebrated in the Yukon
Territories on August 16.

REFERENCES

Acuff, Frank. *How to do business with anyone anywhere in the world.* New York: AMACOM, 1993.

Chesanow, Neil. *The World-class Executive.* New York: Rawson, 1985.

Condon, Richard. *Good Neighbors: Communicating with the Mexicans.* Yarmouth, ME: Intercultural Press, 1985.

Culturgrams. Provo, UT: David M. Kennedy Center for International Studies, Brigham Young University, 1993.

Devine, Elizabeth and Nancy L. Braganti. *The Travelers' Guide to Latin American Customs and Manners.* New York: St. Martin's Press, 1988.

Foster, Dean Allen. *Bargaining Across Borders.* New York: McGraw-Hill, 1992.

Gratton, Michael. *French Canadians: An Outsider's Inside Look at Quebec.* Toronto: Key Porter Books, 1992.

Harris, Philip R. and Robert T. Moran. *Managing Cultural Differences.* Third edition. Houston: Gulf, 1991.

Hiller, Harry H. Canadian Society: A Macro Analysis. Second edition. Scarborough, Canada: Prentiss-Hall Canada, 1991.

Malcolm, Andrew H. *The Canadians.* New York: Times Books, 1985.

Marchant, Gary. *Canada.* Oakland, CA: Compass American Guides, 1991.

Morris, Jan. *O Canada: Travels in an Unknown Country.* New York: HarperCollins, 1990.

Ricks, David A. *Blunders in International Business.* Blackwell: Cambridge, MA, 1993.

Riding, Alan. *Distant Neighbors: A Portrait of the Mexicans.* New York: Alfred A knopf, 1985.

Rossman, Marlene L. *The International Businesswoman of the 90's.* New York: Praeger, 1986.

Snowdon, Sandra. *The Global Edge.* New York: Simon and Schuster, 1985.

Staines, David (ed). *The Forty-ninth and Other Parallels: Contemporary Canadian Perspectives.* Amherst, MA: The University of Massachusetts Press, 1986.

INDEX

I'D LIKE TO HEAR FROM YOU!

Do you have a story or anecdote about your international experiences you'd like to share with me? Or maybe you'd like to comment on parts of this book that you find especially true and relevant (or, for that matter, totally false or trivial). I'd like to hear from you! Please write me at:

Mary Murray Bosrock
International Education Systems
Suite 313
26 East Exchange Street
St. Paul, MN 55101
tel. (612) 227-2052
fax. (612) 223-8383

Thanks so much, and always remember to *Put Your Best Foot Forward*!

—Mary Murray Bosrock

If we include your story in any of our future books we will send you a complete set of the *Put Your Best Foot Forward* series.

Products Available from
IES

- *Put Your Best Foot Forward - Asia*

- *Put Your Best Foot Forward - Europe*

- *Put Your Best Foot Forward - Mexico/Canada*

- *Put Your Best Foot Forward - Russia*

TO ORDER:
TEL. (612) 227-2052   FAX. (612) 223-8383

OR MAIL TO:
INTERNATIONAL EDUCATION SYSTEMS
SUITE 313
26 EAST EXCHANGE STREET
SAINT PAUL, MN 55101

Quantity	Title	Price	Total*
_____	Put Your Best Foot Forward - Asia	19.95	_____
_____	Put Your Best Foot Forward - Europe	22.95	_____
_____	Put Your Best Foot Forward - Mexico/Canada	14.95	_____
_____	Put Your Best Foot Forward - Russia	11.95	_____
		Total enclosed	_____

Name and Title   _____

Company   _____

Address _____

_____

Phone _____   Fax _____

* NOTE : Shipping and Handling not included. Call or fax for shipping charges.
We can ship to your customers worldwide.